MW00778159

HUDSON BEND
and the
Birth of Lake Travis

HUDSON BEND

— and the —

Birth of Lake Travis

Transforming the Hills
West of Austin

Carole McIntosh Sikes

THE
History
PRESS

Site work in preparation for damming the Colorado River at Marshall Ford. Work began by erecting a tower from which to string a cable and transport equipment. *Courtesy Lower Colorado River Corporate Archives, W00380.*

Published by The History Press
Charleston, SC 29403
www.historypress.net

Cover images courtesy of the author's collection and the Lower Colorado River Authority
(LCRA) Corporate Archives.

First published 2014

ISBN 978.1.5402.2369.2

Library of Congress CIP data applied for.

This book is dedicated to the memory of my parents, Georgia Bassett McIntosh and Sidney Carroll "Mac" McIntosh, and to my husband and companion along the way, Charles Thomas Sikes.

Contents

CONTENTS

Preface

This collection of essays reflects my interest in the history of Hudson Bend. The evolution in this area, of which I am a witness, is described from a personal perspective.

For a prehistory account of the native people of Central Texas, as well as some of the early settlers who predate the founding of Lakeway, I recommend the first three chapters of Professor Lewis Carlson's book entitled *Lakeway: A Hill Country Community*.

The major migrations along the Colorado River in Texas began with the Comanche Indians prior to the arrival of white settlers. For purposes of this book, I begin with stories about these first white settlers in Hudson Bend (1854–1889) seeking land grants along the river in the new state of Texas. They began the second migration into the area, followed by a third, smaller but no less important one in the late 1930s. Men called "cedar choppers" came with their axes to clear the land in preparation for a sixty-one-mile-long lake. Two thousand more workers came to construct a dam on the river. These men were eager and grateful to claim jobs that were scarce during the Great Depression. The completion of Mansfield Dam (1941) displaced the subsistence farmers and ranchers who were left along the river. They were the later generations, children and grandchildren of the first settlers. They had experienced droughts and floods, civil war, depression and, finally, displacement from the land.

When World War II ended, a magnificent dam stood in the river, creating a beautiful, long lake in the hills west of Austin. A new generation of weekend residents came to the area for the recreational opportunities on Lake Travis (1940–60). These "weekenders" were the fourth migration. Finally, there was the establishment of many permanent residences and amenities, creating an ongoing fifth migration that is accelerating into the twenty-first century.

As a former columnist for the *Lake Travis View*, a weekly newspaper, I have included interviews and excerpts from those columns in the Appendix. They were entitled "In Hudson Bend" and were written in the late 1990s. Also included are descriptions and comments about some of the organizations and amenities that have been established in the area over the years.

Although the dam at Marshall Ford displaced many landowners who were descendents of the early settlers, it provided hydroelectric power and considerable relief from the all-too-frequent flooding. For seventy-five years, I have witnessed these changes, becoming a permanent resident in 1990. Several books have been written about the lives of the early settlers in Austin and in the hills west of town. However, to my knowledge, this is the first account that covers the rich history of the Hudson Bend area on Lake Travis from its founding to the present day.

Acknowledgements

With so many people to thank, I start with those who read my first draft, giving me the courage to continue: Charles Sikes, Lewis Carlson, Mary Lankford and Louann Temple. I'm grateful to my son, Stuart Bassett Sikes, for technical help and to my daughter, Laura Sikes Barrow, for proofreading. I could not have completed this book without my friend Ann Dolce, whose technical skills, especially scanning photographs, reached far beyond my capabilities.

Thanks for e-mail and telephone conversations and contributions from writers Margie Crisp, Elaine Perkins, Mike Cox and Michael Barnes, writer at the *Austin American Statesman*. I was offered help in so many ways from John Chapman, of the Hudson Bend Colony Neighborhood Association; Morgan McMillian, chief librarian at the Lake Travis Library; Bob Woods, manager at the Austin Yacht Club; Deborah Gernes, director of the Travis County WCID #17, and her assistant, Linda Sandlin; Ana Clark at the Texas Historical Commission; the Reverend Michael Wycoff, rector of St. Luke's on the Lake; and fire chief Robert Abbott.

Help when collecting photographs came from Ann Dolce and the Austin History Center; John Schooley at LCRA; Mike Boston at the Lakeway Heritage Center; Lonnie Moore of Volente; Vance Naumann and Liz Chapman of the Lake Travis Marina Association; Genny Kercheville of the Friends of Nameless School; and Tommy Cain at La Hacienda Realtors.

Most especially, I thank Christen Thompson, commissioning editor, and the other editors at The History Press in Charleston, South Carolina.

Introduction

I was told that my first automobile excursion was in a 1935 Plymouth in my mother's arms. The roads were unpaved and primitive, and the land west of Austin was sparsely populated. Driving from Austin with my parents and my aunt Bonnie and uncle Fred Hopkins, we went to see the unfinished dam at Marshall Ford. My engineer father was especially interested in the design and construction of the dam and excited about the changes the new lake would make in the land twenty miles west of town. He imagined weekend and summer cottages surrounding the lake.

This was the first of many excursions to Lake Travis and Hudson Bend in particular. After almost a lifetime of weekends at Lake Travis, first with parents and later with my husband and children, Charles and I decided to become permanent residents. It was Christmas 1990, and we were just in time to experience the flood that would raise the fluctuating lake, considered full at 681 feet above sea level, to its highest level yet, 709 feet. In my deceased parents' retirement home, to which we had moved, we watched neighbors canoe almost to our doorway. We were safe and dry because our house is above the spillway level of the dam. It is difficult to imagine water ever flooding our home; however, the authorities now have raised the possible flood level from 714 feet to 722. Perhaps we will see more lakefront homes built on stilts in future years. But after seven years of drought that began in 2008, levels of the two fluctuating lakes that serve as principal reservoirs for Central Texas are now only 35 percent full.

Georgia and baby Carole at the dam site, circa 1935. *Author's collection.*

Opposite, top: The Mansfield Dam powerhouse was completed in 1940. Rail tracks ran alongside Ranch Road 620, bringing shipments of supplies and materials to the construction site. The tracks were removed, and the used railroad ties were sold. *Courtesy LCRA Corporate Archives, W01271.*

Opposite, bottom: The tower and track used for transporting equipment, materials and supplies. In the background is Hudson Bend on the south shore and the hills north of the river, 1937. *Courtesy of LCRA Corporate Archives, W01243.*

Shortly after moving to our lake home, I was given the opportunity to write a column for the *Lake Travis View*. Much of the material in this book has been retrieved from my columns, "In Hudson Bend." The chapters in this book are actually essays meant to be appreciated separately. Generally, the order is chronological and listed by subject. The stories contain my memories of early Lake Travis, as well as collected stories from many sources about earlier inhabitants. There are tales of Comanche Indians and some of the first white settlers along the Colorado River, stories about the old farms and ranches and the new dam. There are revelations about the people attempting to work the land along the Colorado River who later were displaced by a new lake and the influx of "weekenders" excited about the recreational opportunities. World War II had ended, and people were ready to celebrate a new life of peace and progress.

A supervisor and construction workers at the dam site preparing to cable supplies and equipment to the work location, 1937. *Courtesy of LCRA Corporate Archives, W01242.*

Plans for the new lake and the construction of the dam west of Austin began in 1937 before the beginning of World War II. Alongside the curving, steep and narrow roadway leading to the dam's site was a railroad for transporting heavy equipment and supplies. After the dam was completed and the railroad dismantled, the discarded, square-cut wooden railroad ties were purchased and used in the construction of many of the weekend cabins that were built on the banks of the new lake.

Construction of the dam produced a population of about two thousand, mostly young men eager for work because people still were recovering from the Great Depression of the 1930s. There were no towns or small settlements in which the workers could live, so a community of dormitory-style housing was provided on land located at the east end of the dam. Marshall Ford Bar and Grill provided libation and rudimentary food. The Bar, as it was called, continued to thrive even after the dam was completed and most of the workers had left. For the new population of weekenders, it became the watering hole and place to get a hamburger on Sunday evenings

A construction worker with a hose wetting the fresh cement atop a finished section of the dam. The lake is beginning to fill behind the dam. *Courtesy of LCRA Corporate Archive, W01067.*

before returning home from activities on the new lake. Unfortunately, it was destroyed by fire and no longer exists.

The widow of a man who had helped construct the dam told me of a tragic accident. Two days after Christmas, on December 27, 1939, Asa Grumbles of Bee Cave, Texas, who was thirty-two, slipped and fell into a cavity that was being filled with tons of concrete. He could not be rescued, and it wasn't possible to retrieve his body. All that his fellow workers were able to do was watch in horror.

The dam was officially completed in 1943, but hydroelectric generation began in 1941. Private automobiles were not allowed to use the two-track roadway on top of the dam until the war ended in 1945. There was fear of saboteurs because our nation was at war with Germany and Japan. Now we call them terrorists, and we know what car bombs and airplanes used as missiles can do. But it was not until the twin towers in New York City were destroyed in 2001 that our nation experienced what local authorities had feared during World War II.

In 1935, our car of sightseers crossed the river on the low-water bridge below the dam and then drove up the steep hill with hairpin turns and switchbacks to reach the primitive, unpaved road in Hudson Bend. At the end of that road, we forded the river and drove to the north shore to see the location of Anderson Mill in Cypress Creek. The old water-driven mill had processed the corn for early settlers to make cornbread. During the Civil War, it had produced gunpowder for the Confederacy.

I was five years old in 1939, when my father and his partner Hugh Webb were planning a subdivision for summer cottages on the proposed lake at Hudson Bend, twenty-two miles from Austin. My father, S.C. "Mac" McIntosh, was a civil engineer working for the Railroad Commission of Texas, and Hugh Webb was an accountant in the state treasurer's office. Webb learned about real estate when working for a bank in Dallas, and McIntosh had laid out subdivisions in Duncan, Oklahoma, and around White Rock Lake in Dallas, Texas. They understood that when the dam was completed at Marshall Ford on the Colorado River, a sixty-one-mile lake would be created that would be even grander, wilder and longer than Lake Austin. Looking for property to buy, they located Joe and Emeline Hudson Williams's old cotton farm at the end of the Hudson Bend Road. The farm appeared deserted. Joe and Emeline Williams were deceased, but they found Henry Williams, a reclusive son, still living in the old farmhouse.

My father told about many Saturdays when he and Mr. Webb, as I called him, would drive out to sit with "old man" Henry Williams on the front porch of the home where he had been raised. The men shared a bottle of bourbon brought from town. I don't know how many weekends or how many bottles of bourbon it took for these two men in their forties to persuade Henry Williams that he and his nine siblings should sell the farm. Nor do I know where Henry went when he left the old farmhouse in which Emeline and Joe Williams had raised their family of ten children. Hugh Webb was responsible for getting Henry Williams to fix a price for the deserted farm. It must have been a considerable chore getting all of his siblings together to agree on a price and to sign the deed, but he did. And in April 1939, the Williams farmland was conveyed to S.C. McIntosh; Fred Hopkins, brother-in-law of McIntosh; and Hugh Webb and his co-worker, Goddard Edwards. Approximately $9,000 had to be raised to make the purchase, so the two founders of the property arranged for a six months' note and invited the two partners to join them. The four were delighted and relieved when the newly created Lower Colorado River Authority (LCRA) purchased an easement to flood half of the seven-hundred-acre farm.

. Men called cedar choppers cleared a wide band of juniper and other trees around the proposed shoreline of the reservoir. The fluctuating lake would help protect the Central Texas hill country against devastating floods, and it would

The new owners of the Hudson Bend property that was formerly the Joe and Emeline Williams farm—Hugh Webb (left) and S.C. McIntosh, 1939. *Author's collection.*

store water and generate hydroelectric power. There were no bulldozers or heavy equipment doing the work of clearing trees. It was done by men with axes who had experienced the Great Depression and were happy to travel wherever there was work to be done.

I loved going out to Joe and Emeline Williams's old farmhouse on the Colorado River. My father and Hugh Webb liked nothing better than to put on their old clothes and worn-out shoes and clear their land. When Mother and I drove out with my dad to the old farmhouse, Mr. Webb and Grace Caruthers usually would be there. Grace was also a state employee, but on weekends she served as the legal secretary for the men's land development project. She loved to work alongside the men, while Mother and I were in charge of spreading the picnic lunch on the table that Mac had fashioned from scrap lumber found around the old house.

Georgia McIntosh, my mother, sat on a folding camp chair reading while waiting to leave the lake area and get back to civilization. There were no furnishings in the dilapidated, unpainted house because it was to be demolished

to make way for the proposed subdivision of lake cottages when the dam was completed. I was allowed to explore the farmhouse and its perimeter. As long as I stayed within shouting distance of my mother, I could satisfy my curiosity. Much to my unhappiness, she never let me go down into the storm shelter that was hollowed out of the ground near the old house.

Like many of the early Texas farmhouses, the Williams house had been constructed to accommodate the parents and their children in two rooms separated by a wide breezeway, or "dog run," open on both ends. It had a tin roof and was constructed with square nails. One room had a stone fireplace for cooking, and I can imagine a very large table for dining. The other room was for sleeping. A porch across the front of the house helped protect the family from the strong summer sun. It and the dog run provided space for the older children to sleep.

When my dad took a little time out from surveying the proposed lots to do some fishing, he would take me with him to the water. And when I was old enough, only about six, he would let me hike with him and Mr. Webb to survey the land they were dividing into lots. Occasionally, to make me feel important, he

McIntosh and his young daughter, Carole, fishing on a cove in the partially filled lake, circa 1939. *Author's collection.*

Opposite, top: The Bohls' cabin was restored and moved to a location on Highway 71 in Bee Cave, Texas. The Hudson Bend farmhouse was a larger timber and dog run house. It was demolished before the dam was completed and the lake was filled. *Author's collection.*

Opposite, bottom: A detail of a dog run and Fachwerk house construction that is common to early German immigrant homes. *Author's collection.*

would let me hold the surveyor's pole marked with distances while he pretended to check a sighting through his scope.

Much of the dreaming and planning for the new subdivision was done late on Sunday afternoons at the Marshall Ford Bar and Grill located near the dam. I was allowed inside only because I was accompanied by an adult. I remember some local youngsters on their own coming to one of the sets of double screen doors with money to buy Cokes. The bartender took some Coca-Colas from one of the big iceboxes behind the long wooden bar and delivered them to the boys waiting outside with their nickels. Yes, five cents would buy a soft drink, and thirty-five cents could purchase a hamburger!

The bar and restaurant had several sets of double doors across the front of the building with advertizing for Butter Crust Bread painted on the screens. Only two were used for entry, and the screen doors would squeak when opened and bang when closed. Because there was no air-conditioning, all were left open for ventilation during the warm months. The best place to be was in the breeze by a door watching the big Wurlitzer that was spinning out country music. Some of the adult couples would glide and step across the hardwood floor to the beat and swing of the music. The men may have been workers on the dam who lived in the camp nearby on Ranch Road 620. Watching the dancers was entertaining for a six-year-old, and I was delighted when Daddy gave me nickels to feed the Wurlitzer jukebox.

When I would return to the table to sit in a ladder-back chair that looked like it might topple over backward, I would be uncomfortable. The scratchy cowhide seat and the tall, straight back would make my back ache. The only relief was looking at the neon beer signs behind the bar. I especially liked the Pearl sign. It had colored lights and a bubbling brook moving across it.

A vacant parking lot marks the place where the Marshall Ford Bar stood before it burned to the ground. It was located just east of the dam on Highway 620, next to what is now Marshall Ford Foodmart. The same brown and cream-colored stones, laid on edge, were used to build the bar, the grocery store, some little one-room cabins and the Hugheses' stone house across the road. The Hughes family owned and occupied much of the land east of the dam at that time.

Georgia didn't especially enjoy those times in the country when my father and his partner were planning the conversion of their goat pasture, as they called it, into a subdivision for weekend cottages on the new lake. I remember Mother saying to my father, "Mac, you go on out this Saturday. Then maybe we'll all go out tomorrow after Carole's Sunday school is over." Even after my father had returned from World War II and I was a teenager with social interests, she used me as her excuse for staying in the new home we built in Austin's Tarrytown subdivision.

Part One

Early Settlers in Hudson Bend

Geography and the River

The Central Texas hill country is unlike all other parts of the state. The eastern part of the state is akin to Louisiana, with tall pine trees and a more humid environment. North Texas experiences colder winters and an occasional snow. On the southern border of Texas are the Gulf Coast and the Rio Grande River, and to the west are the mountains of the Big Bend National Park. In the southern and western plains beyond San Antonio are vast ranch lands with fewer trees—mostly live oak, scrub oak and mesquite—and varieties of vegetation that thrive in warmer temperatures. Austin is the seat of state government and home to the University of Texas. It is located where the flat coastal plains break along the Balcones Fault line to form hills. The terrain rises and stretches out west to create the higher and drier desert plains from which the Hollywood version of Texas was made.

Unlike the Colorado River that begins in Colorado and travels to California, our Texas Colorado River is the longest river contained within a single state. Its many creeks and tributaries drew the Native American tribes of Comanche, Lipan Apache, Tonkawa and Kiowa. The Spanish explorers came through Texas, leaving us with horses and possibly the feral hogs that have become such a nuisance. During the second half of the nineteenth century, early settlers came to the unpopulated hills and the fertile bottomland along the river. When dams were built, the highland lakes were created, displacing the farmers and attracting weekend residents and, finally, full-time inhabitants. Today, we are told that 70 to 170 newcomers arrive daily in central Texas to enjoy warm winters and hot summers, a more stable economy and, undoubtedly, the lakes and the hills.

In the late 1990s, when writing my "In Hudson Bend" columns for the weekly *Lake Travis View*, I became curious about the Colorado River's headwaters. My husband and I decided to search. We were returning home from New Mexico, passing through the flat, red, sandy terrain near Lubbock and Lamesa, Texas. Lamesa is appropriately named because the Spanish word *mesa* means "flat table." Not much could be seen against the horizon on the high, flat plain except a few scattered farmhouses and barns, long irrigation devices, oil and gas well pumps beside storage tanks and an occasional tree. Revenues from oil and gas have made it possible for many of the local landowners to irrigate their land and become gentlemen farmers rather than hardscrabble farmers like the early settlers in Hudson Bend.

Within a triangle formed by Lubbock at the top, Lamesa to the south and Snyder to the east, we found the source of our Texas Colorado River. Thankfully, it had rained and some ground water was visible, otherwise

The headwaters of the Texas Colorado River are located in West Texas near Lubbock. The runoff from rains into creeks and the water from springs created the first named reservoir, Lake Thomas, 1995. *Author's collection.*

we would not have believed that this was the insignificant beginning of the mighty river that provides drinking water, recreational pleasure and irrigation to so many central and south-costal Texans.[1]

Traveling on U.S. Highway 180 connecting Lamesa with Snyder, the most astonishingly radical change in the terrain occurs. The flat, straight road drops from the high, sandy mesa into a rolling, rocky basin with long-running gashes, called draws. "Draw" is a western term for a naturally occurring drainage ditch or geological indention in the land that gathers rainwater and eventually channels it into a creek or a river. A draw can be dry and benign most of the time, but it can become a raging torrent of water after a heavy rain. Without any transition, the flat, irrigated farmland instantly gave way to rugged ranch land looking like something in a John Wayne movie. Prior to our arrival in the area, there had been enough rain to fill some of the channels, convincing us that we were, indeed, witnessing the beginning of our Colorado River.

In the middle of this basin, we found Lake J.B. Thomas, a shallow, dammed reservoir filled with water dyed red from runoff from the sandy farmlands above it on the mesa. The first of the Highland Lakes on the Colorado River was barely more than a muddy pond and seemed more like a silt-catching pond than a recreational lake. There were a few simple cabins

A draw is defined as a gulley or ravine that water drains into or through. Draws are often dry and can become filled with raging water after a rainstorm. *Author's collection.*

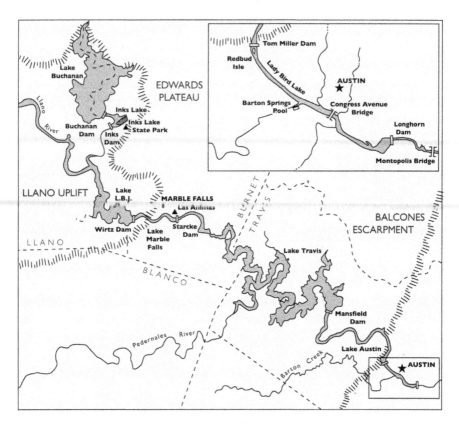

Map of the Highland Lakes. *Reprinted with permission from* River of Contrasts: The Texas Colorado *(Austin: Texas A&M University Press, 2012), by Margie Crisp.*

set back several football field lengths from the lake. Located near one of the cabins, a pier made of cedar poles stood high above cracked red earth, indicating to us that Lake Thomas fluctuates wildly depending on rainfall in the area.[2]

Water in the upper Colorado River takes on the color of the soils over which it flows. The name Colorado denotes a ruddy reddish color. However, after the river moves through two other named reservoirs, E.V. Spence and Ivie, and then over limestone cliffs and around rocky hills, it becomes clearer and cleaner. From Lake Buchanan, on the Llano uplift, the river travels on to other Central Texas lakes—Inks Lake, Lake LBJ, Lake Marble Falls, Lake Travis, Lake Austin and Lady Bird Lake. From Austin, the river heads southeast and finally into Matagorda Bay and the Gulf of Mexico.[3]

Hudson Bend: Now and Then

Twenty-first-century Hudson Bend has a uniquely diverse population. It never has ascribed to being a town or even a village. As the city of Austin encroaches on its western hills, becoming larger and more urbane, the new "Hudson Benders" remain fiercely independent and adverse to restrictive codes. Streets are paved but not curbed. The 1950s lake houses and weekend fishing cabins are replaced with lakeside residences and family homes, but still there is the sense of living in the country. There are new RV parks and old mobile homes among the live oak and cedar trees shared with deer, fox and coyotes. Blue heron, chaparral, cardinal and all varieties of migratory birds fly overhead. Today, the peninsula of land accommodates four or five marinas and numerous private docks, but public access to the lake is diminishing. During this time of drought, there are no public boat ramps available for visiting boaters.

In the mid-nineteenth century, courageous farming families left their homes for a frontier that demanded hard work and promised danger. They were eager to acquire the land in Hudson Bend to make a better life for themselves and their children. On the subject of families moving west, a handsome southern gentleman with deep roots in Memphis, Tennessee, once said to me, "Those folks traveling west who could read stopped in Tennessee, the others went on to Texas." There is definitely truth in his statement because many of the early documents for the exchange of land in Texas were signed with *X*'s by those who could neither read nor write.

After Texans fought to become free from Mexico, Texas became a sovereign nation before becoming a state on December 29, 1845. It was the new frontier. Texas enacted the first homestead legislation in America, declaring that homesteads could not be seized for debt. Land grants were available until 1889, when there was no more land in the public domain.[4] The process involved finding the land, having it surveyed, filing an affidavit for preemption with the county and living on the land for three years. After that, a certificate of occupancy could be granted.

Imagine hills covered with tall, thick pasture grass rather than land choked with what we call cedar trees, actually a variety of juniper. The land along the river was fertile, with soil deep enough to grow cotton and corn. The trees along the banks of the river were tall cypress and pecan trees. At the end of dirt wagon trails, there were simple timber and rock homes built above the river to protect against the all-too-frequent flooding.

Map of early Texas land grants in Hudson Bend. *Courtesy of Texas Historical Commission.*

There were abundant fish to catch, and wild turkeys, squirrels and sometimes bears to hunt. However, goldenrod, beggar's lice, bull nettle, scorpions and many snakes inhabited the land.

Although the land along the river was fertile, the soil on the slopes and hillsides was shallow, growing only cactus and scrub vegetation. Rocks in abundance were used in building homes, barns and fences. Cedar trees were cut and used for fences, foundations and doorframes in the homes made of rocks and logs.

Indians were still a threat in the late nineteenth century, but raids on the settlers and their homes were subsiding. However, horses, livestock and crops were still vulnerable. A writer for the online magazine TexasEscape.com tells a 1930s story about Hudson Bend. It is retold here with permission from the author, Mike

Cox. Perhaps the story is about a great-grandson of Wiley Hudson's because, had Hudson lived until 1930, he would have been 107 years old.

> *By the time Hudson had grandchildren, the families living in the hills west of Austin no longer feared raiding Comanches. But well into the twentieth century, a rifle still hung above every mantle, and a Texan learned how to shoot early.*
>
> *A boy was shooting the family's .22-caliber single-shot gun. He was admonished by the elder Hudson to stay clear of the two skittish mules that were hitched to a wagon loaded with corn to be hauled to Anderson Mill. When a bullet whistled past the mules, they jumped and ran wildly for a gate, overturning the wagon, breaking the gate and spilling corn in a great mound on the ground.*
>
> *In anger, Hudson grabbed the gun from the boy and smashed it against a pecan tree, bending the barrel. To this, the cocky boy responded, "Now I can shoot around corners!"*
>
> *At that, Hudson retrieved the bent rifle and hurled it out into the river.*

As I write this, Lake Travis is at its second-lowest level, approaching the record low-lake level since the Lower Colorado River Authority (LCRA)) has been keeping records. It is unlikely, but perhaps someone could find an old bent shotgun buried under the silt of many years.

In the broadest part of our lake near the dam, when the lake is low, we can see islands. The exposed land is called Sometimes Islands. As the water continues to recede, these islands become a strip of land known by early settlers as Horseshoe Bend. The nine hundred acres of land were submerged when the dam was completed, and a huge basin of water covered Horseshoe Bend completely. That bend in the river can be detected only when the water level of Lake Travis recedes to around 630 feet above sea level. Many times, a less severe drought has caused islands to appear. Twice in my lifetime have the islands become a peninsula. Then it is possible to imagine how the early settlers, riding their horses or driving their oxen, could use this land as passage to the river. When traveling into Austin on horseback from Hudson Bend, there were several options for crossing the river. If pulling a wagon, the preferred route was to travel across Horseshoe Bend to Marshall Ford and into Austin.

There have always been droughts and floods on the Colorado River. For the subsistence farmers along the river, floods were arguably the worst situation of the two. There was no defense against the raging water sweeping away the corn and cotton fields, the kitchen gardens planted in the fertile bottomlands and even buildings too near the water's edge.

Horseshoe Bend was the first bend in the river north of Marshall Ford. It was named for its shape. When the river became a lake, the land was covered. However, when the fluctuating lake recedes, islands appear. *Courtesy of LCRA Corporate Archives, W00129.*

An aerial photo of the land mass know as Horseshoe Bend, on the same side of the river as Hudson Bend. *Courtesy of LCRA Corporate Archives.*

Usually, the floods were preceded by several years of hardship due to drought. The early settlers had to haul water from the river, which at times and in places could be almost dry. Today, Central Texas lakes, bereft of adequate rainfall at least since 2008, are managed by the Lower Colorado River Authority (LCRA). The LCRA was created in the 1930s, putting forth the taming of the river as a primary reason for acquiring federal money to build dams. The river authority governs the releases of water through the dams built along the river. Lakes Travis and Buchanan provide water to rice growers and other users downstream. Their levels fluctuate while the lakes in between are kept at a constant level. Lake Travis is determined to be full at 681 feet above sea level. Today, in 2014, it is only one-third full. The Sometimes Islands in Lake Travis have been exposed for three and a half years, and the water releases for rice growers near the Texas coast have ceased for the past two years.

Rains are sure to follow, and then the problem is likely to be flooding. In 1957, many days of rain broke the drought of record. I was teaching young students, eleven and twelve years old, who had never seen sheets of rain coming down for days. For them, it was as rare as a Central Texas snowstorm. A less severe drought was followed by a flood in 1991. The lake rose quickly to a record high of 709 feet, causing many houses in Hudson Bend to be flooded. When lake levels rise above 681 feet, the U.S. Army Corp of Engineers and the Federal Emergency Management Authority (FEMA) take over management from LCRA.

Water is our most precious natural resource. The management of it is necessary to sustain life. When Native Americans experienced droughts along the rivers, their populations had to move or wither away. Along the Colorado River near the Hudson Bend, the Comanche Indians prevailed for many years until the white settlers arrived in the mid-nineteenth century.

Even after the white man's defenses began to discourage the Indian raids, traveling into town for provisions was dangerous. Comanche Indians still roamed and marauded in the hills west of Austin, hoping to steal horses and confiscate goods. However, it was necessary to make the trip to buy nails and wire and to supplement the meager provisions that families struggled to raise on their farms. Often, wives and children were left alone overnight with only a shotgun for protection.

Today, there is a street overlooking the big basin of Lake Travis called Comanche Trail. It leads to the Oasis Restaurant high on a cliff above the lake. The Oasis is one of Austin's favorite tourist destinations for watching the sunset while sipping margaritas and dining on TexMex food. At this location in the 1950s, I remember a modest summer house where Georgia McIntosh, Mae Brown and other ladies would enjoy lazy afternoons playing a game of bridge while looking out over the lake that now covers the trails made by the Indians and the settlers in those early days.

One hundred years after Wiley and Catherine Hudson settled on the bend in the river that was given the Hudson name, their children and grandchildren have died and descendants are scattered. A beautiful lake covers the farmland. After World War II, much of Hudson Bend was subdivided, and the lakefront lots were selling to new owners for $200. The Hudson Bend Road became lined with pastures fenced with cedar posts and "bob" wire, as it was called. White-faced cattle belonging to Beby's Ranch looked up at the new owners driving the Hudson Bend Road to their weekend houses.

Owners of lakefront lots, on what is now Eck Lane, drove over cattle guards and through bump gates on McCormick's Ranch to reach their properties. Bump gates were double gates that would close both the entrances and exits of the ranch roads until nudged by the vehicle seeking to pass through. If a car attempted to push through a bump gate too fast, the gate on the opposite side of the center pole would spin around and slam into the rear of the car, delighting children who might be in the backseat of the vehicle.

There were fishing cabins to rent at Brillville and boat docks on what later was called Paradise Cove. Brillville was part of Arno Brill's Ranch, and it became another early Hudson Bend subdivision. Because the family fishing camp was to be called Brillville, he restricted it from serving alcoholic beverages. Brill's daughter Nellie married John Connally. Young John would borrow his father-in-law's truck for his campaigning trips around the state. Texas governor John Connally may have taken the truck idea from Lyndon Johnson's playbook about the best way to appeal to voters living in the rural areas of Texas. It is understandable that Arno Brill was not happy with his son-in-law when the borrowed the truck was returned to the ranch with the gasoline gauge on empty. The name Brillville is almost forgotten, and today the area is better known as Rocky Ridge on Paradise Cove.

Before the Travis Landing subdivision in Hudson Bend was developed, prominent Austin businessman Joe Cocke owned the property. One of his three daughters was an equestrian. Terry Jo kept her horses there for several years, driving out from Austin frequently to exercise them.

Among the characters in Texas history, there were two governors whose names could induce chuckles. They were Pappy O'Daniels and "Ma" Fergerson. In 1925, Ma Fergerson was the first woman elected governor in the United States, followed shortly after by another woman elected to that office in Wyoming. Later, in the 1950s, Texas had a Governor Jester and a state treasurer Jesse James

It was Jesse James, the state treasurer of Texas and not the notorious renegade, who purchased Goddard Edwards's and J.H. Edwards's interests in the Hudson Bend Colony subdivision in 1945. He created the Lake Travis Lodges and Boat Docks at the end of Hudson Bend Road. He would instruct his assistants at the capitol building to call him after telling anyone who was looking for him that he would be back in his office in forty-five minutes. That was the time it took to drive from Hudson Bend into downtown Austin. His

The Lake Travis Lodges during the flood of 1957. Floods occur on the Highland Lake chain frequently after droughts. *Author's collection.*

rental lodges were made from salvaged army officer barracks, or Quonset huts, and covered with native rock. They were built so close to the water that they were flooded several times before being demolished. Located on higher ground, his small store sold gasoline, fish bait and necessary provisions for the new lot owners and the weekend fishermen and their families renting the cabins.

Atop the cedar fence posts along the Hudson Bend Road, weekend fishermen displayed heads of the big catfish they had caught as trophies for all to see as they traveled back into town. Oliver Sponberg, a weekend resident of Hudson Bend, told me, "In 1940, I had the biggest boat on Lake

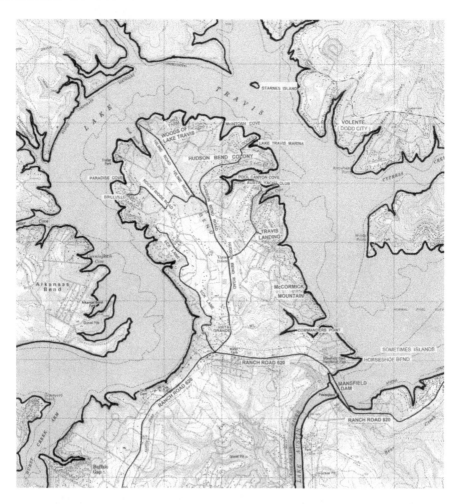

A Geological Survey topographical map of Hudson Bend with additions by the author. *Author's collection.*

Travis. It was a sixteen-foot aluminum fishing boat with an outboard motor that had no reverse." Oliver's wife, Anita Disch Sponberg, was a daughter of "Uncle Billy Disch" of local baseball fame. The University of Texas named its baseball field Disch-Faulk Field.

Anita discovered the square nails from the old Joe and Emeline Williams farmhouse on their lakefront lot in the Hudson Bend Colony subdivision. The storm shelter was found on the Betsy and George Dykes's adjacent lake property.

It seemed a long time before the ski boats, sailboats and big yachts took over the lake. As late as the mid-1950s, I remember water skiing behind young Judd Miller's aluminum fishing boat with an outboard motor so strong that it lifted the boat's bow out of the water until finally it would plane. The water was cool and clear and smooth under the shadow of the huge new dam.

The first sailboats on Lake Travis were either kept on trailers or moored in many of the coves on the lake. The Austin Yacht Club was founded in the 1950s. Its members initially met in one of Jesse James's rock cabins located on higher ground near his store. Later, the club bought Beacon Lodges at the mouth of Pool Canyon Cove and installed sailboat slips for members. It still occupies that location and sponsors numerous regattas for its members.

Driving down Hudson Bend Road today, one finds that the fenced pastures, with bump gates and cattle guards, have been replaced by everything from a sail maker's shop, rows of boats stored on their trailers, old cars offering used auto parts, the Hudson Bend Grocery Store, Los Pinos Restaurant, a Taqueria, a do-it-yourself laundry, a meat market offering deer processing and an RV park to a pool hall, plus other entrepreneurial attempts of all kinds. I call the area Downtown Hudson Bend, although "the Bend" never has been and never will be a town. These commercial endeavors render it impossible to visualize the natural beauty of the virgin land that seduced early settlers to travel this wagon trail to the riverfront.

The Wiley and Catherine Hudson Family

It is difficult to imagine what Wiley and Catherine Hudson saw when they came to Central Texas, but by all accounts, it must have been beautiful virgin land. Wiley K. Hudson was born in Arkansas in 1825. Family legend has it that the Hudson family, or some of them, moved to Missouri. In 1837, Wiley,

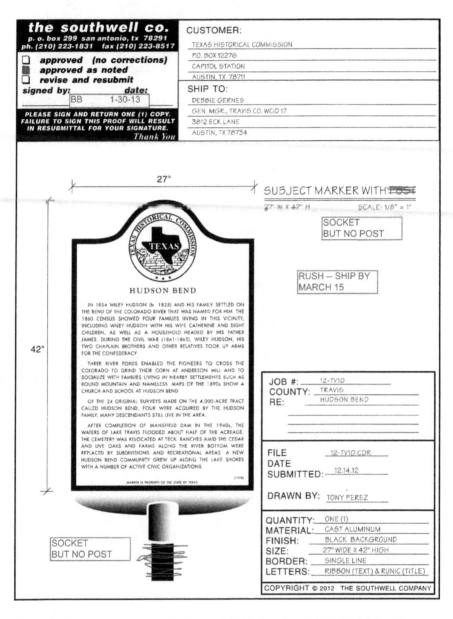

An application for a replacement for the original Hudson Bend Historical Marker that was hit by a car, destroyed and stolen, 2013. *Courtesy of Texas Historical Commission.*

as a boy of twelve or thirteen years of age, traveled with his family in a wagon pulled by oxen to the land called Texas.[5] Apparently, the family returned to Arkansas. Wiley was married when he was eighteen or nineteen years old. His bride, Catherine, was a year younger. Their first child, James Franklin Hudson, was born in Arkansas. The couple eventually had eight children.

Although we don't know where the Hudson family had been in Texas, Wiley must have cherished the memory. Sometime between 1844 and 1848, he returned to Texas with his wife and firstborn child. Wiley filed an affidavit for preemption of land in Travis County in the year 1854. He and his family are believed to be the first white settlers in the area named Hudson Bend. After the required three years of living on his land, he was granted a certificate of occupancy on February 17, 1857.

The land grant system in Texas was simple. After a county board of commissioners reviewed and granted an application, the land was taken out of the public domain. The grantee engaged a surveyor and marked his plot. The survey notes were certified and sent to the state land commissioner, who issued a patent. The institution of preemptive, or squatter's, rights enabled men to pay fifty cents per acre up to 320 acres. Land continued to be preempted until 1889, when there was no more public domain in the state.[6]

In 1840, Travis County was formed from the wilderness in the new state of Texas. Despite the hardships that the young Wiley Hudson family must have endured, others in the family followed seeking land grants along the Texas Colorado River. Four families and twenty-eight people appeared in the 1860 census of Travis County. It was recorded that Wiley Hudson was a thirty-five-year-old farmer from Arkansas; his wife, Catherine, was thirty-four, from Tennessee; and their eight children ranged in age from six months to sixteen years. The eldest son, James Franklin Hudson, was born in Arkansas in 1844, and their second child, Jane, was born in Texas in 1848.

Other families in the Hudson Bend at that time were Caleb Nunnery, a farmer from South Carolina; his wife, Martha, from Tennessee; and their six-year-old son, William. Farmer James Forbes was from North Carolina, and his wife, Elizabeth, was from Tennessee. Their eight children ranged in age from one to eighteen. Wiley's father, James Harris Hudson, a fifty-six-year-old farmer from Tennessee, arrived in 1858 with his wife, Sarah, also from Tennessee. They brought three of their children ranging in age from seventeen to twenty-three years.

By the end of the nineteenth century, twenty-four land grants had been made on the approximately four thousand acres in Hudson Bend. Today, much of those four thousand acres are normally under water or subject to flooding. Among those very early Hudson Bend land surveys for grants, listed in Travis County records, are names that will be familiar to those reading this and the later essays in the book.

W.H. or Henry Hudson (born 1858), a son of Wiley and Catherine, was on the list of early land surveys in Hudson Bend. He acquired land adjacent to his father's, receiving his patent on his land on February 7, 1883. Wiley's son, J. A. Hudson, or Joseph Alexander Hudson (1855–1924), was married to Tophenia Harris. His certificate of occupancy is dated July 1881. Later, Joseph moved to Hamilton, Texas. After the death of his wife in 1900, he returned to live with his children on the other side of the river but was buried in the Hudson Bend Cemetery. Later, graves had to be moved because the new lake would cover the cemetery. Joseph's reinterment was in the Teck Cemetery. For more about Joseph Alexander and other Hudsons, see interviews by J.M. Owens in the Appendix of this book.

Tophenia Hudson's father, J.H. Harris, was an early settler in the bend. He had a homestead on present-day Webb Lane in the Hudson Bend Colony Subdivision Number Two. It was in the vicinity of today's Keller Marina and the Austin Yacht Club, near the mouth of Pool Canyon Cove. In the early 1950s, state treasurer Jesse James made the Harris home his weekend house.

There are two versions of the "Grampa" Harris adventure that is considered to be the last skirmish between Comanches and the white settlers in Hudson Bend. The following version was told to me by George Zintincho, a former neighbor in the Hudson Bend Colony.

Grampa Harris was traveling alone into Austin for provisions. He heard Indians behind him in the brush. Knowing that they rarely attacked groups of persons traveling together, he began to shout. "Come on men! Hurry up—we've got to get on into town before dark. Come on! Hurry up!" His loud encouragement to his imaginary companions discouraged the Indians, and they departed. Grampa Harris survived to tell his tale, either this version or the following, to all who would listen.

This next version is the more often repeated, slightly different one told by John C. Hudson, son of Joseph and Tophenia Harris Hudson to J.M. "Mulky" Owens. It is recorded by Owens in the Texas Historical Commission's documents and also recited in *A Hill Country Paradise, Travis Country and Its Early Settlers*, by author Elaine Perkins, a Bee Cave, Texas resident.

Grampa Harris, father-in-law of Joseph Hudson, went out one morning to look for some calves that had strayed. He trailed them across the Colorado River at about where St. Luke's Episcopal Church on the Lake now stands. As Grampa Harris started up the draw, he came upon ten or twelve Indians. He immediately dismounted and headed for the nearby brush, where he knew the Indians would be reluctant to follow. The Indians were shooting at him, and one of the arrows hit the stock of Harris's gun and knocked a chunk out of it. He then decided that to survive, he would have to shoot some of the Indians. One of the Indians mounted Harris's horse and was trying to ride off with it. Apparently, the horse didn't like the smell of the Indian and began trying to buck him off. About that time, someone appeared on the bluff above the draw and began to call out for Harris. Thinking reinforcements had come, the Indians jumped on their horses and rode away, taking Harris's horse and saddle with them. Since that time, this draw has been known as Defeat Hollow.

Take your pick. I like the Mulky and Elaine version. However, Grampa Harris might have told a version similar to Zentinko's story because it makes him, not the stranger on the cliff, the hero.

When Wiley's parents, James Harris Hudson and his wife, Sarah, left their home and moved to Texas to join their son, it was 1858. They brought their three younger sons, one daughter and twenty horses. Their homestead on the bend of the Colorado River was opposite Sandy Creek. It included a stone house, a working farm and honeybees. From the Texas Historical Commission's documents, we know birthdates for the children of James and Sarah Hudson. Wiley was born in 1825; John, in 1831; Edward, in 1837; Joseph, in 1841; and daughter Jeoinetta, in 1843. It is recorded that on July 16, 1862, Wiley's brother, Edward Hudson, paid the state treasurer eighty-eight dollars for his land. He would have been twenty-five years old.[7]

When a tribe of Comanche Indians attempted to steal James Hudson's horses, neighbors joined the Hudson men in tracking the thieves. One horse was killed in the exchange of fire, but all of the others were rounded up by their rescuers and returned to the senior Hudson. Deadly attacks by Indians were abating. However, the whole of Central Texas still was very wary of Indian raids during the second half of the nineteenth century. The Comanche Indians had earned a terrible reputation for scalping adults, kidnapping women and children and often killing them, as well as the men with whom they fought. Jeffery Kerr, an Austin physician, collected stories of difficulty and courage during some of these early years. His book, *The Republic of Austin*, highlights the decade between 1832 and 1844. His stories have notations of when and where in Austin so many of the Indian skirmishes took place.

Wiley and Catherine Hudson's eldest daughter, Jane, was born in 1848. She married Tom (T.H.) Sylvester, whose land was on the western edge of Hudson Bend across the river from C.H. Sylvester. Although Tom's land was in Hudson Bend, C.H. Sylvester's land was in Arkansas Bend.[8]

Five in this photo can be identified as adult children of Wiley and Catherine Hudson. *From left to right*: Henry Gregg Hudson; Harriet Hudson Haydon; (Bathsheba Hudson or "Bash" Milam, offspring or perhaps sister of Wiley Hudson); Ann Hudson Toungate; Joseph Alexander Hudson; and Emeline Hudson Williams. *Courtesy of the Austin History Center.*

Five of Wiley and Catherine Hudson's progeny appear as adults in a photo with Bathsheba or "Bash" Hudson Milam, and they were all residents of the area.

Bathsheba was married twice, first to a man named Gilcrease. She had been a schoolteacher in Arkansas and married a second time to widower Burris Milam. Their union eventually totaled nine children, adding five to his four by his deceased first wife. In 1859, one year after James Harris Hudson left Arkansas with horses and headed to Texas to join his son Wiley, Burris and Bathsheba made the same arduous wagon ride with four children. They encountered difficulty with Indians and an overturned wagon with the children inside. However, all survived and made it to their destination on the Colorado River. Burris bought land in Hudson Bend but later moved his large family upstream to where the Pedernales River and the Colorado River intersect.

Daughter Harriet Hudson (1861–1936) married Burgess Haydon (1856–1939). They are buried in the Fitzhugh Cemetery.[9] Although the 1937 survey map shows only a W.H. Haydon property, the Burgess Haydon family lived on land that was near the beginning of the primitive wagon trail that is now

From left to right, top row: Rosie, Wiley, James J., Charlie, Alvie, John and Evie Haydon. *Second row*: Minnie Bailey Haydon, unidentified child, Bessie Combs Haydon and a Crumley daughter-in-law. *Third row*: Burgess Haydon and Harriet Hudson Haydon. Fourth row: Herman Brown and children, Minnie Haydon Brown and Lillie Haydon Crumley. *Courtesy of Austin History Center.*

Hudson Bend Road. They raised a large family in a home that burned. As a child, I remember riding with my family down Hudson Bend Road past the barn and the adjacent windmill. Before the lake was created, it was a very pastoral scene, with tall grasses and the purple hills in the distant background. Today, the barn is surrounded by boats on trailers, recreational vehicles and other evidence of nonessential possessions.

Virgil C. Haydon, a grandson of Wiley and Catherine, was in possession of the Hudson family Bible when state highway engineer J.M. "Mulky" Owens was researching Hudson history. Virgil Haydon told Owens that his father had been married once before he married Harriet Hudson.

In 1977, Owens was responsible for acquiring the original historical marker that gave some of the history of the Hudson family. The original marker was sponsored by the Hudson Bend Lion's Club, dedicated to its late president, Floyd C. Olsen, and located on land donated by Paul Keller. It is believed that the land was originally the Haydon homestead, and the old red tin barn, still barely standing in 2014, was theirs.

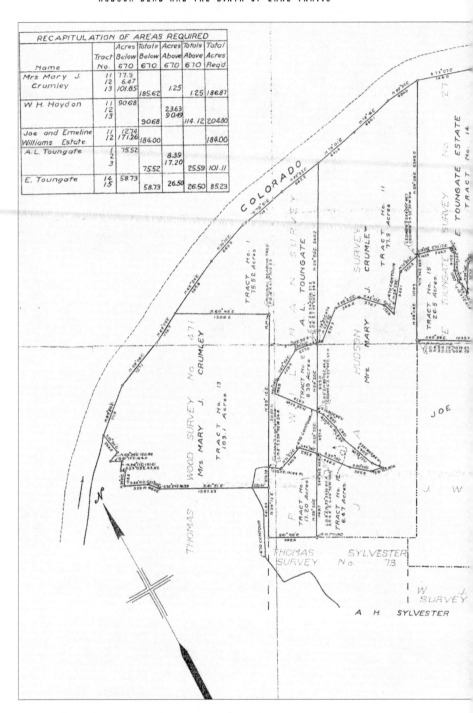

RECAPITULATION OF AREAS REQUIRED						
Name	Tract No.	Acres Below 670	Totals Below 670	Acres Above 670	Totals Above 670	Total Acres Req'd
Mrs Mary J. Crumley	11 12 13	77.3 6.47 101.85	185.62	1.25	1.25	186.87
W. H. Haydon	11 12 13	90.68	90.68	23.63 90.49	114.12	204.80
Joe and Emeline Williams Estate	11 12	12.74 171.26	184.00			184.00
A. L. Toungate	1 2 3	75.52	75.52	8.39 17.20	25.59	101.11
E. Toungate	14 15	58.73	58.73	26.50	26.50	85.23

The 1937 Right of Way Survey was prepared in order to identify the owners of the land so that easements to flood the property could be purchased when the river became a lake. *Author's collection.*

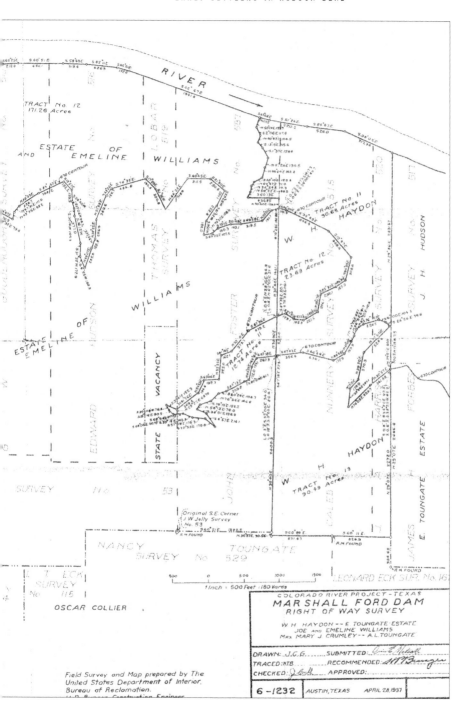

COLORADO RIVER PROJECT-TEXAS
MARSHALL FORD DAM
RIGHT OF WAY SURVEY

W. H. HAYDON -- E. TOUNGATE ESTATE
JOE and EMELINE WILLIAMS
Mrs. MARY J. CRUMLEY -- A. L. TOUNGATE

DRAWN: J.C.G.	SUBMITTED:	
TRACED: NTB	RECOMMENDED:	
CHECKED:	APPROVED:	
6-1232	AUSTIN, TEXAS	APRIL 28, 1937

Field Survey and Map prepared by The
United States Department of Interior,
Bureau of Reclamation.

Several years ago while driving the Hudson Bend Road, I saw a woman beside her car; she had knocked the marker from its post. I deeply regret not stopping along with the others gathered there because no one secured the historical marker, and it was stolen. However, in 2013, the Hudson Bend Garden Club and our Travis County Water District procured the replacement that stands on Hudson Bend Road today. The cost was $1,400.

Another daughter of Wiley and Catherine was Emeline Hudson, born 1849. Her husband, Joe Williams, acquired seven hundred acres on the river. This included the Harris land plus several other properties in Hudson Bend, primarily the Edward Hudson, G.W. Goodenough, Thomas Lobar and John Foster surveys along the river. In 1939, the Williams land was purchased by S.C. McIntosh and Hugh Webb. It became the Hudson Bend Colony Subdivision.

Later, McIntosh and Webb purchased the Toungate's adjoining two hundred acres. It was undeveloped until 1971, when Hugh Webb's heirs bought the McIntosh interest and sold it to Jim Vier and his partners. Vier created The Woods of Lake Travis subdivision.

Ephriam Toungate (1849–1935) married Ann Hudson (1856–1939). Ann was another of Wiley and Catherine's daughters. She may have been the daughter listed as "Caza, 5 years old" in the 1860 census.[10] Interviews with later Hudsons could not confirm this. Ephraim and Ann may have been living on the Toungate property that adjoined the Williams farm. However, I believe Ann and Ephriam might also have lived on the Toungate tract that was across the river from Anderson Mill. Thomas Anderson, Ephraim Toungate and Nick Hayes built the mill from huge cypress trees, near the rushing water in Cypress Creek, on the north shore. Ephriam was buried in the Fitzhugh Cemetery.

Anderson Mill was a gathering place for area residents traveling to the mill with wagonloads of corn to be ground. They stayed overnight, visiting with other families camping in the area, while waiting their turns to have their corn turned into meal. During the Civil War, the men used the mill to make gunpowder for the South. The old mill in Cypress Creek ceased to operate, and it was inundated by the new lake. However, the North Shore Garden Club constructed a replica near Volente, Texas.

Some of the courageous men who settled in Hudson Bend, fought with Comanches and endured other hardships to establish a community in the wilds of Texas, felt compelled to take up arms and fight in the Civil War (1861–1865). Wiley Hudson's two younger, bachelor brothers, Edward and John, served as chaplains in the war.

Portrait of Ephriam and Ann Hudson Toungate. (Ann may have been Caza, the five-year-old listed in the 1860 census.) *Courtesy of Austin History Center.*

The Toungate home (1890 or 1891). *From left to right*: Arch Toungate with horses; Manuel, William (Bud) and Bertha Toungate; Lizzie Toungate Marshall; Edward Marshall (holding Burnie Marshall); and Columbus, Ellie, Ephraim and Franklin Toungate. The remaining names are illegible except the last adult, identified as Ann Hudson Toungate. *Courtesy Austin History Center.*

According to records and research by J.M. "Mulky" Owens,[11] Edward Hudson was wounded and crippled in the Civil War. He and his brother John Hudson are buried in Round Rock, Texas. Wiley Hudson's sons-in-law, Burris Milam and Joe Williams, also served in the Confederate army; however, there are conflicting stories regarding Wiley's service, or lack thereof. Several of these accounts claim that he served the Confederacy and was seriously wounded but made it back to Austin, where he died. Another story is that he refused to enlist, and several men from Austin apprehended him, dragged him to the river and drowned him. This is unconfirmed, but it is true that Rebel renegades living in Austin and other parts of Central Texas stalked, persecuted and even killed Union supporters.

The war changed lives. Wiley died in Austin and did not return to Hudson Bend. Edward Hudson sold his land to Archer Morrison on December 10, 1870, for eighty dollars, slightly less than he had paid, and moved to Round Rock, Texas. He and his brother John lived and died there.

In 1965, the Reverend Edward Hudson and Reverend John Hudson, bachelor brothers of Wiley Hudson, were honored in nearby Round Rock, Texas. A historical marker, dedicated to the memory of these brothers, was placed at the entrance to the Old Settlers Association reunion grounds at the southwest quadrant of the intersection of Interstate Highway 35 and Ranch Road 620 in Round Rock, Texas. The marker in Round Rock reads as follows:

> *Confederate Chaplains Rev. Edward Hudson and Rev. John Hudson*
> *Brothers, teachers, Presbyterian ministers. Came to Texas from Arkansas, 1856.*
> *Worked and lived in this county. Both are buried in Round Rock Cemetery.*
>
> *In the Civil War, Rev. Edward Hudson, in March 1862, joined Co.*
> *G, 6th regiment, Confederate Army. Wounded Oct. 1862, in Battle of*
> *Corinth, was made Chaplain afterwards to succeed man killed in that*
> *same Battle. In Aug. 1864, on duty in Georgia, was shot and critically*
> *wounded. Though crippled, preached and taught in various Texas counties*
> *until shortly before his death, Aug. 17 1877.*
>
> *Rev. John Hudson enlisted in April, 1862, in Co. H, 19th Texas*
> *Calvary. Commissioned in March 1863. He served as Chaplain for the*
> *rest of the war. After preaching here for many years, died Feb. 22, 1914.*
>
> *On same pay and rations as privates, a Chaplain had multiple duties.*
> *Religious services, teaching men to read and write, counseling, sick visits,*
> *handling the mail, writing letters and reading to illiterates, removal of dead*
> *and wounded from the battlefield, baptisms, funerals. The Hudsons may have*
> *been the only Texas Brothers enrolled in this valuable Confederate service.*

Other Early Settlers

By 1860, there were four Hudson families in the Hudson Bend, and many other families were settling along the river on both the south and north shores of the Colorado River. We can be certain these early settlers saw beauty and promise. Today, the landscape is radically changed along this part of the Colorado River, and it will continue to change. Now, whether you live in Hudson Bend, where there are still few restrictions about what can be done, or in the newer areas like Lakeway, where there are abundant admonitions about how one's property must look, Wiley Hudson's hill country has vanished.

Many of the bends in the river were named for these early settlers coming from other states to acquire land along the Colorado River. Emigrants coming from other countries, especially Germany, to Texas

Lois and Charles Schneider fishing in Schneider Cove on Anderson Bend, located upstream from Hudson Bend. A portion of their large ranch was flooded in 1935 before the dam was constructed. *Courtesy of Ann Johnston Dolce.*

arrived at the port in Galveston and traveled on to Austin and other settlements at Fredericksburg and New Braunfels. Some stopped and stayed in Austin. However, many moved up the Colorado River from the newly established capital of Texas to claim land on which to farm or ranch. In addition to Hudson Bend, there are two more bends named for settlers, Anderson Bend and Thurman Bend. Arkansas Bend is named for the area from which the settlers came.

There were other places to ford the river upstream from Marshall Ford, where the new dam would be located in the years to follow. There was Watson Ford, near Big Sandy Creek, and Sylvester Ford on the southwest side of Hudson Bend. T.H. or Tom Sylvester of Hudson Bend owned land directly across the river from C.H. Sylvester, whose land was in Arkansas Bend southwest of Hudson Bend. Stewart Ford was farther upstream and named for the large Stewart family living near Hurst Creek.

The early homesteaders on the rocky terrain worked together to create a community. Families built their houses of cedar and native stone on land above the river that frequently flooded, but they farmed in the fertile soil at the water's edge. Water had to be carried up from the river to their homes. Some dug wells and had crude windmills to pump water for livestock and for home needs. Others constructed stone cisterns to catch rain. Life was difficult, and children had to work alongside their parents. They helped with chores and had little time for learning letters and numbers after gardens were tended, livestock fed, wood cut, fires built and water hauled and boiled for cooking and washing. However, when they were not needed to help with chores, I'm told that they attended a temporary lean-to school in Hudson Bend called Lone Ives School. According to Ernest "Tubby" or "Sonny" Stewart, who was interviewed in 1995, it was the first school in the county, but there were other small, one-room schools in the greater area.[12]

In 1874, after the Civil War ended, James Riley Watson moved with his family to teach in the one-room Hudson Bend School. He was thirty-four years old and taught grownups as well as children. On United States Geological Survey maps made in the 1890s and early 1900s, there was a school and a church at about the center of Hudson Bend. There were other schools in the surrounding areas that were important, not only for educating the children, but also for providing a place for social gatherings.[13]

Listed and appearing on an early land grant map in the Texas Historical Commission's archives is the name Leonard T. Eck. He established a general store that eventually included a post office. The store was located on the main wagon trail south of today's popular Hudson's on the Bend Restaurant. There are three stories about how Mr. Eck's store got the name Teck Store. According to Stewart, "The name above Leonard T. Eck's old store had faded and appeared to read Teck. The name was adopted for the entire area."

Another story that has passed down is simply that people found it difficult to say Eck Store, so they renamed it Teck Store. A third, more pragmatic but less delightful tale, is that the postal service required a four-letter name, so the community became known as Teck.

Home delivery of mail did not immediately come to the area, so the store and post office became a gathering place for neighbors eager for mail. They lived along both sides of the wagon road that we know today as Ranch Road 620. The mail was delivered to Postmaster Eck from Austin on horseback or by horse and buggy from 1900 to 1918. Later, a number of older men and several widows took turns at the job of delivering the mail, in their horse-drawn buggies, to farms and ranches in the Teck area.

The Eck and Stewart families were close friends and eventually were linked. The two families shared an interest in providing schools and in educating the children in the area.

The first Stewarts in the area were Benjamin and Sara Stewart. They came to Texas from Tennessee in 1860. They amassed 1,500 acres of land stretching from the mouth of Hurst Creek downstream toward Hudson Bend. Benjamin K. Stewart (1805–1872) and his wife, Sara, had a son, Bird K. Stewart (1846–1823), who was the father of Albert Kendrick Stewart (1872–1944). In the early 1930s, one of A.K. Stewart's eight children was Ernest C. Stewart (1898–1973), father to my resource and friend the second Ernest "Tubby" Stewart.

It was Grandfather A.K. Stewart who built a two-room school with a cloakroom and privies to accommodate children of the entire Teck community. The Hudson Bend School and the Hurst Creek School were combined, and it was called the Teck School.[14]

Ernest C. Stewart united the two prominent families in the early 1930s, when he married an Eck daughter and later purchased the store and post office from his wife's father, who was Leonard T. Eck Sr. It became the Ernest C. Stewart Store, and Annie Stewart became the postmistress for the Teck community.

The Deaf Band performing in front of the Teck/Stewart Store, circa 1920–30. It had been a general store, post office and a school, within or to the rear of the store. There was a small corral for the schoolchildren's horses. *Official Archives of the Lakeway Heritage Center, Lakeway, Texas, 78734.*

Leonard Eck Jr. and his father were important to the community of Teck. The Eck Store became the Teck Post Office. Hudson Bend and Hurst Creek schools were combined into one, and Leonard Eck Jr. donated land for the new Teck School, circa 1900. *Courtesy Austin History Center.*

It is believed that at one time the school was located in or near the general store and that children living in Hudson Bend and in areas south toward Hurst Creek would walk or ride horses to school, using the corral behind the store. Later, the school was moved to land donated by Leonard T. Eck Jr. and remodeled.

Stewart believed the school built by his grandfather A.K. Stewart was where either the Iguana Grill Restaurant or the Vineyard subdivision is

A page from the Teck School yearbook, 1936. Included are pictures of trustees W.H. Haydon, W.B. Haydon and A.H. Sylvester and Leota Caveness. *Official Archives of the Lakeway Heritage Center, Lakeway, Texas, 78734.*

now located. Lakeway archivist Mike Boston believes that the Teck School, established in 1890, was located on the east side of what is now Ranch Road 620 near the Teck Store, a cotton gin and a small corral. Attending the school were Stewarts, Hudsons, Williamses, Toungates, Haydons, Ecks, Sylvesters and others. Many of these classmates married one another, as did my friend Ernest "Tubby" Stewart's parents. The school closed in 1937, when many families moved from their homes to make way for the new lake.

After Ernest C. Stewart and his wife closed the store, they moved into Austin and operated a motel on South Congress Avenue. This is where my friend Ernest lived, growing up in Austin. Although "Tubby," as a mature adult, was no longer tubby when I met him in the late 1990s, he still answered to that name. As a child, he spent his summers with grandparents in the country and referred to his Grandmother Eck with great affection. I'm wondering if she contributed to her grandson's childhood nickname by baking treats for him.

Descendants of the early settlers, especially the third and fourth generations, gave up farming along the river and relocated to find jobs to better support their families. As children, they had firsthand experience of droughts, floods and all manner of difficulties. The land was poor and overgrazed. The more fertile land along the banks of the river, where their parents and grandparents had grown grain, corn and cotton and where they had collected pecans, figs and wild grapes, was to be inundated. Preparation for the dam at Marshall Ford was underway as early as 1936. Indeed, when the dam was completed, a wide, sixty-one-mile lake destroyed what was left of farming in the area.

The Joe and Emeline Williams Farm

Wiley and Catherine Hudson's daughter Emeline married Joe Williams. Their seven-hundred-acre farm was located just downstream from the bend in the river at the end of the wagon trail that became Hudson Bend Road. It consisted of several adjoining land grants, including the G.W. Goodenough survey, the Edward Hudson survey, the Thomas Lobar survey, the John Foster survey and others.

Emeline Hudson Williams gave birth to at least ten children. She and her husband, Joe, raised them in their two-room home on the banks of the Colorado River. In 1939, when McIntosh and Webb purchased the Williams farmland, the old, abandoned home was still standing. The adult heirs were living elsewhere.

We know that at one time there were cattle on the land, and there must have been milk cows and perhaps goats and sheep. When there were droughts, it was especially difficult to feed and water the livestock. No evidence was found of a well on the Williams land, so water may have been hauled from the river. When children were old enough to help, they were given chores such as hauling water, harvesting the crops and collecting pecans from the tall trees that grew along the river. There were wild grapes and berries to pick, as well as whatever might have been planted in the kitchen gardens. Lone Ives, the lean-to school that the children attended when they weren't needed at home, was marked "school tract" on an early subdivision plat for Hudson Bend Colony Number Two. The tract was located at the end of the draw that became Pool Canyon Cove. A grotto was nearby that may at one time have had water flowing from a spring. All the springs, now surrounded by thirsty cedar trees, have dried up.

We know the work of the subsistence farmers was extremely difficult, but there was socializing among the different communities—Hudson Bend, Hurst Creek and Bee Cave. Usually, it was not difficult to cross the river to join friends or family. A school, established in the 1870s on the north shore, became the meeting place for a wide area. In 1880, the community built a permanent school and applied to establish a post office. Six names were submitted and rejected by the U.S. Postal Service because they were already in use. Finally, the people wrote, "Let it be nameless and be damned." According to the National Archives, the name "Nameless" was accepted, and the post office was established on January 19, 1880. Nameless Road leads to the one-room schoolhouse restored in 2009.[15]

In the 1880s, there was a terrible drought. Gardens dried up, and the stock animals became thin. Several families, including the Williamses, Hudsons, Haydons, Crumleys, Sylvesters, Milams and Toungates, were persuaded by the pastor of the Baptist congregation in Hudson Bend that God was punishing them. It was suggested that they have an old-fashioned camp meeting and pray for forgiveness and for rain. They built a brush arbor on the school grounds, butchered a cow and invited all the neighbors to come and bring food to share.

According to Elaine Perkins,[16] Joe Williams rarely spoke in public, but when all the provisions had been consumed, he made a public statement: "I want this meeting to go on. I have about a hundred head of cattle. If any of them will make beef, go get them."

People kept coming, as did preachers from all around, and the meeting lasted three weeks. We don't know when the drought was broken, but apparently the people found relief and comfort in numbers.

Later generations learned that the land was not really conducive to ranching and farming. Many gave it up and found other places and other ways to live. The abundant and beautiful grasses that Wiley Hudson saw when coming to the area were soon overgrazed and did not return because the soil was too thin. The hillsides were rocky and could not easily sustain many cattle or even goats, which will eat anything, including pants legs and skirt hems. The early homes were rudimentary, like the Williams home. Much of rural Texas was without light and heat until 1937. Stone fireplaces provided the warmth in the winter and were used for cooking and baking all year. If the family owned a smokehouse, meat from a hunt could be smoked and preserved. Because wood was abundant, the hill country people learned to make charcoal. It was made in pits by men called "charcoal burners." Several cords of cedar were put in a pit, covered lightly with dirt to keep out the air and burned for several days; then they were uncovered and bagged.[17]

Smokehouses were used by early settlers as the only way to preserve and store game. This example is believed to have belonged to the Bohl family of Bee Cave, Texas. *Author's collection.*

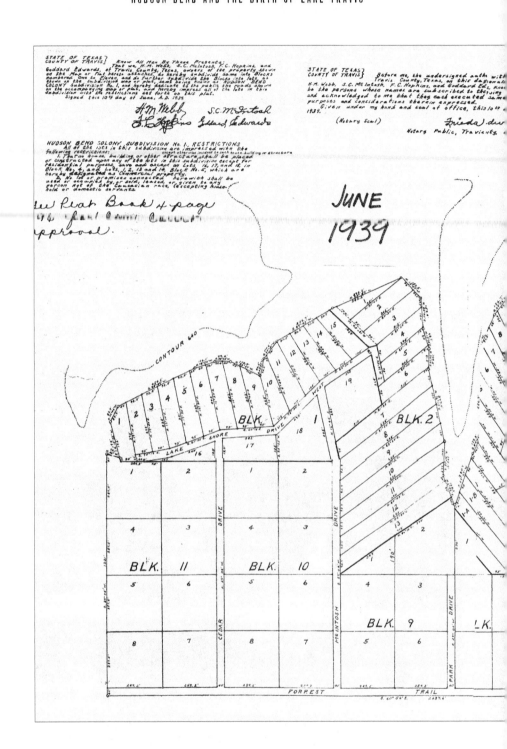

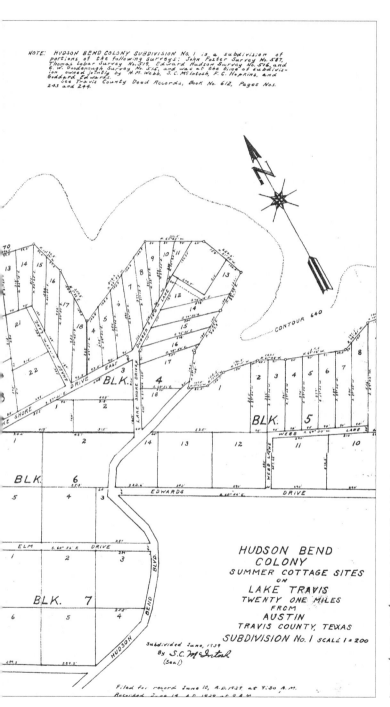

The original
Hudson
Bend Colony
subdivision was
planned by S.C.
McIntosh and
Hugh Webb
on land once
belonging to
Joe Williams.
McIntosh and
Webb purchased
the land from
Joe and Emeline
Hudson Williams's
heirs in 1939.
Author's collection.

In 1939, the adult children of the Joe and Emeline Williams family were scattered. My father, S.C. McIntosh, and his friend Hugh Webb met with Henry Williams on numerous weekends at his family's deserted farmhouse. Finally, in April 1939, Henry was persuaded to sell the family farmland to the two men. The house in which they met had a tin roof and was constructed with square nails. Like many of the early Texas farmhouses, it had accommodated Joe and Emeline and all of their ten children in two rooms. The rooms were separated by a wide breezeway, called a dog run, open on both ends. There was a porch across the front to help cool the house in the summer. The rock fireplace in one of the rooms was for cooking and heating. The second room, across from the dog run, was for sleeping. I expect some of the older children slept in the breezeway and on the porch.[18]

After the farmland was conveyed, the two friends, now partners, immediately began to survey and plat the subdivision for summer cottages on the banks of the proposed Lake Travis. This original plat for the Hudson Bend Colony subdivision, dated 1939, became obsolete when authorities decided to raise the spillway level on the new dam to 714 feet above sea level. Raising the level of the proposed lake caused the planned lakefront lots in the subdivision to be subject to flooding. That necessitated a revision in the plans that my father had no time to complete. Our nation was preparing for war. Although older than the cutoff draft age of forty, he volunteered for service in the U.S. Army Corps of Engineers. As with so many businesses during World War II, the Hudson Bend Colony subdivision in the Texas hill country had to be put on hold.

Fathers and brothers who volunteered or were drafted, as well as a few women who volunteered, were being shipped to training camps. Winston Churchill had been courting President Franklin Roosevelt, hoping to draw our country into the fight against Hitler's aggression. The Japanese bombing of our naval fleet in Pearl Harbor in 1941 achieved that task for him. United States career military personnel and new recruits were quickly deployed to Europe and to the South Pacific and other parts of the world to fight against aggression.

Part Two
A New Vision for the River and the Hills West of Austin

The Dam at Marshall Ford: Changing Lives

Twenty miles from Austin, in a great gorge near a crossing on the Colorado River, a huge dam was being constructed. When it was completed, the beautiful, deep, sixty-one-mile-long reservoir, with crystal clear water running over the limestone cliffs, covered the ford near Marshall's Ranch and many other crossings on the river. A bridge at Lohmann's Crossing was inundated, seriously separating neighbors on the two shores.[19] Tall cypress, sycamore and pecan trees along the riverbanks were swallowed up, yet many still remain in the depths of the lake. Cemeteries had to be moved. Farmlands and homesteads were inundated partially or entirely. Farming families were scattered and had to make new and different lives in new and different places.

We know very little of prehistoric inhabitants in this area except that remains of the Leander Lady were found nearby in the town of that name. Professor Lew Carlson has written about the Clovis nation, which included part of our hill country.[20] History tells us that explorers from Spain, passing through Texas searching for cities of gold, lost many of their horses in skirmishes with the marauding Comanche Indians. For purposes of these stories, I'm going to count the tribes of Comanche, Lipan Apache, Tonkawa and Kiowa as the first of the migrations into our area of Central Texas because much evidence of their habitation was left all along our Colorado

River. We know counties were formed after Texas became a state, bringing a second migration of farmers and ranchers and their families to apply to the counties for grants of land. In our area, these were white settlers primarily from Arkansas and Tennessee.

In 1854, Wiley and Catherine Hudson and their children were settled along the bend in the river named for them. They are recognized as the first permanent white settlers on "the Bend." By the end of the 1870s, Indian tribes were being assigned to reservations by our government, and some individual Indians were slowly integrating into the white man's world. Many of the early farmers and ranchers were leaving, discouraged by frequent floods, droughts and the economic depression of the 1930s. The final exodus of these landholders along the banks of the river came with the completion of the dam and the creation of Lake Travis. The only part of their land that was fertile enough for farming had been inundated.[21]

Preparation for the dam and the new lake created jobs eagerly embraced by a third migration into Central Texas. These were men still recovering from the Great Depression and still looking for work. Men called cedar choppers came with their axes to cut trees and brush in a band along the proposed lake's shoreline. Two thousand construction workers came to build the huge concrete dam at Marshall Ford. Some were young, single men; some were men with families; and others came leaving wives and children behind.

The work done by a Chicago firm on the Hamilton Dam, near Burnet, had been halted for two years. The Insull Corporation was in bankruptcy. However, when construction of these two and the other dams along the river was completed, it brought enormous benefits for Central Texans. Workers had money, the value of land was appreciating and the dams were generating hydroelectric power, bringing light and heat to people and places that before 1937 had neither.

The dam at Marshall Ford is an engineering marvel. Its official opening was in the year 1943, but it was generating electric power in 1941. The

Opposite, top: The dam at Marshall Ford was finished. Horseshoe Bend was inundated when the lake was filled, forming a big basin in which Sometimes Islands appear when the lake recedes, circa 1942. *Courtesy LCRA Corporate Archive, W01194.*

Opposite, bottom: Built in 1931, Lohmann's Bridge, connected the south and north shores of the river. In 1861, John Henry Lohmann settled land on the river near present-day Lakeway. The bridge is now submerged near Lohmans Crossing. *Courtesy of the North Shore Heritage and Cultural Society.*

A worker (lower right) proudly viewing the unfinished Marshall Ford Dam, 1940. The name was changed to Mansfield Dam in 1941 to honor Joseph Jefferson Mansfield, U.S. congressman and chairman of the Rivers, Harbors and Navigation Committee. *Courtesy of LCRA Corporate Archives, W00746.*

Building a dam and impounding a lake. Floodgates were opened to achieve the correct lake level during construction, 1940. *Courtesy LCRA Corporate Archives, W00177.*

completion of it and the dam upstream creating Lake Buchanan took much political maneuvering. Politics at the time dictated that the best stated purpose for securing federal public works money was that the dams would bring relief from flooding. Only because of the work of a few very dedicated and tenacious men in Washington, D.C., and some lucky breaks did the Marshall Ford and Hamilton Dams, later named Mansfield and Buchanan, get completed.

Alvin Wirtz, a Texas state senator from Seguin, was soft-spoken but apparently very influential. He was council to the newly formed Lower

Texas State senator and lawyer from Seguin Alvin Wirtz represented the Lower Colorado River Authority and the Brown and Root Construction Company. He supported young Lyndon Johnson in his run for congressman from the Tenth District of Texas. *Courtesy LCRA Corporate Archives, A00394.*

Colorado River Authority (LCRA), as well as to the Brown and Root Construction Company selected to build the dam at Marshall Ford.

In 1936, the U.S. Department of the Interior's Bureau of Reclamation issued a federal grant to the Brown brothers, Herman and George. They received the first year's portion for the cost of building the dam. The Brown and Root Company also borrowed money to purchase the necessary and costly equipment, hired the workers and began their work on the federal works project at Marshall Ford.

Meanwhile, a bureaucrat in Washington, D.C., discovered an obscure law forbidding the construction of a dam on land that was not owned by the federal government. Texas was a sovereign nation before becoming a state in 1845, so it owned all of its public land, including where the two dams were being constructed.[22]

James P. "Buck" Buchanan was a powerful and confident member of the U.S. House of Representatives from the Tenth District of Texas. He was a favorite of President Franklin Delano Roosevelt, so he believed he could

Congressman J.P. "Buck" Buchanan, member of the U.S. House of Representatives from Texas and a favorite of President Franklin D. Roosevelt. Though he was confident he could resolve the problem of the stalled construction of the dams, he died suddenly. *Courtesy LCRA Corporate Archives, A00303.*

rectify the problem of the obscure law as soon as Congress reconvened. After all, he had asked the president to make federal money available for the completion of Hamilton Dam, in his district, as a birthday gift to him. His request had been granted.

Alas, in February 1937, before acting on his plan for the two dams, Buchanan suffered a heart attack and died. State senator Alvin Wirtz, who not only was politically powerful in the state but also had connections in Washington, supported young Lyndon Johnson to replace Buchanan in the House of Representatives. He believed Johnson could best represent Texas and the two projects underway on the Colorado River. Johnson was not considered likely to win, but win he did.

When the Hamilton Dam was completed, it was renamed Buchanan Dam. In 1941, the dam at Marshall Ford also had a name change to honor Joseph Jefferson Mansfield, congressman from Texas from 1916 until 1947. As chairman of the powerful Rivers, Harbors and Navigation Committee in the House of Representatives, his help was central to the cause.[23]

Lyndon Johnson, kneeling in the lower left of the photograph, celebrating Mansfield Dam with others who had been instrumental in restarting the Colorado River Dam Projects, 1942. *Courtesy of LCRA Corporate Archives, W00057.*

Finally, cars were allowed to drive across the dam instead of traveling across the low-water bridge and up a steep, curving hill to the opposite side of the river. For security reasons, the roadway on top of the dam had been closed until World War II ended. *Courtesy LCRA Corporate Archives, W00781.*

Although Mansfield Dam was officially completed in 1943, for security reasons, the roadway across the top of the dam remained closed during most of World War II. After the war, the two-lane roadway was opened to traffic, making the new lake much more accessible. The low-water bridge and the steeply curving, uphill road had been difficult and dangerous.

The victory in Europe and the two-lane roadway atop the dam encouraged a fourth migration. Men who had a new vision for the land and families who embraced the lake's recreational opportunities were drawn to the area. Abandoned farm and ranch land was traded and subdivided. Weekend cottages and cabins were built on the newly created lots and occupied by those interested in fishing and boating on the new lake.

Lake Travis, and especially the Hudson Bend area, became part of my personal history at a very young age and continues to be to this day. In 1947, my father returned to civilian life and built a lake house on Pool Canyon Cove in the Hudson Bend Colony subdivision. We could be counted among the fourth migration of weekenders grateful for the roadway across the dam and the views of the beautiful new lake.

By 1970, my father was retired. He and my mother sold their home in town, built a retirement home on McIntosh Cove and became permanent

A tall bridge below the dam completed in 1994 to accommodate the increasing traffic. In the background is Hudson Bend. Lake Travis is in flood stage, with floodgates open and releasing water, 1991. *Courtesy LCRA Corporate Archives.*

residents of Hudson Bend on Lake Travis. They lived there for twenty years until they died at ages ninety and ninety-two. Meanwhile, Lakeway, founded in 1963 as a prime resort and retirement community near Austin, was encouraging more supporting businesses in the area. There were a few markets and restaurants and eventually professional services to follow.

In December 1990, my husband and I sold our home in Austin and moved to my deceased parents' retirement home on McIntosh Cove in Hudson Bend. Four years later, in December 1994, we accessed the Hudson Bend Colony via the tall, new, four-lane bridge built between the dam and the low-water bridge. The two-lane roadway atop the dam could no longer accommodate the increased traffic. Once again, it was closed to public traffic in January 1995.

Today, a fifth migration is arriving as I write this. According to the *Austin American Statesman* dated August 10, 2013, more than seventy people come to live in Austin every day. The myriad new homes continuing to be built in, around and all over Austin are filled with young singles and families flocking to Central Texas from adjacent cities and far-away states and nations. To accommodate the influx, new downtown condominiums and apartment towers have changed our skyline. Suburban shopping centers and malls, with connecting apartment complexes, have appeared. Complete new neighborhoods of homes filled with newcomers seem to appear everywhere there are vacant tracts of land.

The city of Lakeway is no longer a retirement community but a thriving city of fourteen thousand and growing. With the establishment of the Lake Travis Independent School District, children in Hudson Bend, Apache Shores, Bee Cave and the Hurst Creek/Lakeway areas are no longer bused to Dripping Springs schools. In the older subdivisions like those in the Hudson Bend, small weekend cabins and lake houses are being demolished and replaced with larger, permanent homes. The laid-back Austin of my childhood is no more, and the hills are alive with traffic.

World War II

When I was seven, a world that I knew nothing about was at war, and our nation was on the brink of joining our allies in Europe to fight Nazi Germany. In 1941, our naval fleet stationed in Pearl Harbor was bombed by Hitler's allies, the Japanese. The circumstances of my family—and indeed, those of families all over America—changed suddenly and radically. The cutoff age for being drafted into the armed services was forty-five. Although my father was beyond that age, he volunteered. As an army engineer, he was sent to train at an army camp in Louisiana and then on to the Aleutian Islands in Alaska. As a captain and later a major, he and his men were building supply lines, roads, bridges and rail lines to prepare for a possible invasion by Japan into Alaska. Gratefully, this never happened, and Major McIntosh returned to his wife and child and to a beautiful, full Lake Travis in 1946.

Before leaving for service, my father and Hugh Webb took two new partners to help with financing and planning for their Lake Travis subdivision, which they named Hudson Bend Colony. Mac's brother-in-law, Fred Hopkins, and Webb's associate in the state capitol building, Goddard Edwards, were passive but compatible partners. However, near the end of the war, Hopkins sold his interest to Edwards's father and left for Houston to start a commercial kitchen design business. In 1945, Goddard Edwards and his father sold their interests in the Hudson Bend Colony to Jesse James, the Texas state treasurer in whose office the younger Edwards and Hugh

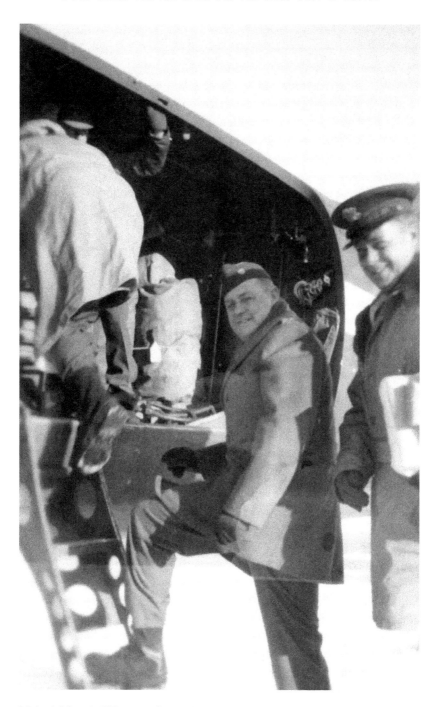

Major McIntosh, U.S. Army Corps of Engineers, boarding a plane for the Aleutian Islands of Alaska. His battalion was building supply lines, roads, bridges and rail lines in preparation for a possible invasion by Japan. *Author's collection.*

Aerial view of the bend named for Wiley Hudson. Pool Canyon Cove is in the foreground, and Devil's Canyon, in the background, is across the partially filled lake from Hudson Bend, 1941. *Author's collection.*

Webb worked. James now owned one-half interest, and unfortunately, the new partnership was not working well.

My father's 1939 subdivision design had to be abandoned when it was determined that the overflow spillway level on the dam would be raised to 714 feet above sea level. This meant that during times of flooding, the fluctuating lake might rise to a higher level than originally planned, covering a tier of the proposed waterfront lots in the original plat of the Hudson Bend Colony. Lakefront lots would need to be deeper so that houses could be set back and safer from flooding. The decision to raise the level of the new dam was made with good reason. Pressure from floodwaters in Lake Austin had twice broken the Tom Miller Dam.

During World War II, there was not much economic activity on Lake Travis or anywhere in the nation if it didn't relate to the war effort. Occasionally, a lot was sold, and Major McIntosh in Alaska was called on to create a partial plat from his notes and drawings. When it was completed and sent to Austin, his partner, Hugh Webb, took the section that was platted to the Travis County Courthouse to be filed. Consequently, the Hudson Bend Colony was platted in several separate sections and at different times, even after the war ended.

The massive dam was renamed Mansfield Dam after its completion. It is 279 feet high, 7,089 feet long and 213 feet thick at the base. With the war ending, the two-lane road atop the dam was opened to traffic. It was exciting to ride far above the newly formed lake, enjoying a wonderful view of the grand basin. As I write this, the low-water bridge still remains, but the precariously steep road up the hill on the west side of the river was abandoned and is now overgrown.

Approximately half of the Williamses' seven-hundred-acre farm was inundated. When the river became a lake, the hill across the river from Hudson Bend became Starnes Island. The sailors loved the island as a picnic destination. However, it became known as Rattlesnake Island because many snakes had retreated to higher ground there.

In the 1930s, across the river from Hudson Bend, there was a hill that would later become an island. This photo was taken from the north shore near present-day Volente, with Hudson Bend in the background. *Courtesy of Lonnie Moore.*

Aerial view of Hudson Bend on Lake Travis with Sandy Creek and Starnes Island, circa 1941. It was also known as Rattlesnake Island because the snakes retreated to higher ground there when the land became inundated. *Author's collection.*

Unfortunately, Mac was not home when the new lake was impounded. I still have the letter that his friend and partner Hugh Webb wrote to him describing what he had seen and how he felt when watching the rugged land fill with water to create a beautiful new lake. Here are excerpts from the letter dated December 1942:

> *Dear Mac:*
>
> *Your somewhat belated but none the less appreciated and interesting letter [was] received a day or two ago. Of all the places in this wide world to which our brave soldiers are being sent to unfurl the Stars and Stripes and stop the bloodthirsty Japs and Germans, it seems to me you are very fortunate indeed in being sent to the "land of the midnight sun" and the Aurora Borealis...and when you return to civilization you will find new wonders to behold, from which you will never again want to roam.*

The rough and rocky shores of Lake Travis have been transformed, and the places you once knew are no more—they are all covered over in our own made to order fashion with crystal clear, blue water, which magnifies gorgeous sunsets and makes more beautiful and impressive the big yellow moon as it slowly rises in splendor to cast its very obliging yellow beams across the hills for lovers to bill and coo. All of the ugly places have been completely erased, and only the beauty spots remain, justifying your far sighted vision and for you to enjoy as your tender, youthful years lengthen into a complacent old age. But judging from the picture you recently sent to Georgia, I must not be talking to you, for that picture betrays the youth.

My idea is that the country, in which you are now so pleasantly encamped, is no doubt very beautiful…but every day it is the same old view…snow does not change in color—its always white. It will sooner or later grow monotonous, and you will then understand and appreciate that it's just a place to go and see, while your own home sweet home on Lake Travis is a place to live and die.

Remember too, the same old sun…[in Alaska]…also paints its pictures in variegated colors across the ever changing green clad hills of Lake Travis. Here, as the seasons come and go, and the leaves change their colors, by reason of which the sunsets change their colors too, there will be no monotony, and nowhere on earth will you ever see sunsets more beautiful.

Bull aside—our business affairs are at a standstill. While matters are not as I would have them, still I believe you realize how hard it was to accomplish anything with divergent ideas and opinions, some of which were flavored with hostility. I suppose to wait for your return is all we can do. [24]

[signed] *Hugh Webb*

After the completion of the Buchanan and Mansfield Dams, a chain of three pass-through lakes was created by a series of dams among them. A wild Central Texas river was tamed. It became possible to harness the all-too-frequent, destructive floods while providing for the storage of water and the production of electricity. Upstream from Lake Travis is Starke Dam, holding waters in Lake Marble Falls; then Wirtz Dam, holding Lake LBJ; then Inks Dam, holding Inks Lake; and, finally, Buchanan Dam, holding its fluctuating lake. Controlled releases from Lake Buchanan keep the flow-through lakes at constant levels.

After the War Ended

After the war ended, there was pride in what the nation had accomplished. People had energy and ambition to create productive lives that would fulfill their prewar dreams.[25] Most importantly, families were together again. Although far too many were grieving about fathers and sons and friends missing, lost in the war, the nation could now heal and move forward.

The McIntosh family of three was together again. We were among the families photographed and featured in the *Austin American Statesman*'s special section about servicemen returning to their homes in Austin. However, adjustments had to be made. My father was not the same daddy I remembered. For him, his child of age seven was now entering the teen years. I realize that my parents made adjustments of which I was not aware. My mother, Georgia, had "worn the pants" in the family for several years. She now was expected to defer to Mac in most instances.

Georgia insisted that Mac dispose of the old, unsightly flatbed truck he had left in the backyard of our home in town. Before leaving to enlist in the army, he had purchased it while clearing cedar from the Lake Travis land. Because it was a wonderful curiosity for all of my neighborhood friends who played on it, my mother had forgiven him. He especially had been exonerated when she had learned that she could use the "C" (commercial vehicle) gasoline ration coupons along with the "A" stamps to provide gas for our 1940 Chevrolet during the war.

The McIntosh family was featured, along with other reunited families, in the *Austin American Statesman*, 1946. *Author's collection.*

Our family made a fresh start with a move into our newly constructed house on the lot that Mother had selected and purchased with my father's allotment sent to her while he was away. My father turned his attention to his beloved Lake Travis. However, because state treasurer Jesse James had purchased both my uncle's and his employee's interests, he was now the major partner in the Hudson Bend Colony subdivision project. Unfortunately, he had not been imprinted with the goals and ideas of the two originators of the subdivision. Had he been more understanding, he might have been an easier partner. The solution to this situation was to divide the remaining lots and tracts among the three partners, enabling each man to work autonomously.

With our new home in town occupying my mother's time, my father began building their weekend house on Pool Canyon Cove at Lake Travis. Many, if not most, of the roads leading to the lake were unpaved and dusty. Most of the construction of our lake house was done by my father; what he could not do himself, he contracted. Many of the materials were army surplus purchased from Camp Swift in Bastrop, Texas. The wide pine paneling had been U.S. Army mess hall tabletops. The house had one large room with a huge fireplace built by a local stonemason. He had learned his trade from his father, who had been an earlier resident of the hill country. I remember my mother telling about the day she tuned a radio to a country music station inside the house where he was working. With his Texas drawl, he said, "That were sure purdy music, Miz McIntosh."

In addition to the main room that had beds for winter sleeping, there was a bath, a kitchen and a screened porch for summer sleeping. In 1949, as with many houses, there was no air conditioning, but a huge, noisy attic fan kept us reasonably cool in the summertime. On winter weekends, butane space heaters, along with the wood-burning fireplace, kept us warm. Electric service was from the City of Austin. We had a well but brought drinking water from town. The back-entry porch had peeled cedar poles lifting the roof and a cargo canoe hanging from the ceiling. Frequently, Jesse James's cows came to look in our windows.

In 1950, we had a Southwestern Bell party line phone with a crank to turn when calling out and a ring of three longs and two shorts to notify us of an incoming call. This was progress from the early Bee Cave telephone system. In the earlier days, subscribers were responsible for installing and maintaining the lines strung from trees and fence posts to their farmhouses. Johnson's Trading Post in Bee Cave was the message center for those without phones, and its generators provided power for the private party line system. Early subscribers on the Hudson Bend line were Henry Hudson, Jim Hudson and Bob Marshall. The Bee Cave line included a Joe Beck, several Bohls, Walter Maul and Bud Toungate. The Teck line included the Teck Store, a Mr. Eck and several Haydons, Stewarts, Sylvesters and Crumleys. The Reimers were on the Hamilton Pool line. These families were descendants of the earliest settlers in the area. An operator would place and perhaps monitor their calls, not unlike the comedian Lilly Thomlin's depiction of "ringy-dingy" calls on the party line.

The Pool Canyon Cove, in front of our weekend house, was deep and cool and wonderful for swimming. Eventually, we had a boat dock. I remember swimming along the shore one afternoon when my father, working on our dock, began motioning and shouting for me to stop swimming and get out of the water. I stopped swimming but responded as a typical teenager with: "Why?" A snake was swimming at a right angle to my path in the water. Perhaps my splash would have driven the snake away, but had I seen him, I would have been terrified.

Truly a happy camper, Mac spent all of his weekends at Lake Travis, working on our lake house, meeting new lot owners and often helping others any way that he could. The new subdivision was filling with weekend cottages, fishing cabins and an occasional permanent residence.

Hudson Bend was pastoral and beautiful, with native grasses and the lake with distant hills in the background. Still, there were bump gates and cattle guards. Cows and a few horses grazed behind barbed-wire fences. On the cedar fence posts, fishermen occasionally left the heads of large catfish as trophies for all to see as evidence of a successful weekend fishing trip.

There still were vacant tracts of land yet to be divided into lots. My father and his friend Hugh Webb decided to raise adorable, curly, white, wool-producing Angora goats. One weekend, we noticed that a mother goat was ignoring her baby, not allowing it to nurse. University students, while enjoying a picnic, had been petting and playing with the kid. The mother goat would no longer claim it. I begged until it was agreed that we would take the little goat into town and raise it on a bottle. Each weekday morning, my father and I would drive off to work and to school, leaving Mother sitting on the back porch with the baby goat and its bottle. I think for revenge, she named it Stinky. He learned to walk on the flat but narrow wooden rail atop our backyard fence. However, it was a wet spring, and the St. Augustine grass lawn caused Stinky's hooves to rot. We returned him to the rocky soil in Hudson Bend. Alas, he had never seen another goat, or even his own reflection, and was terrified of the strange-looking creatures that were his own kind.

The subdivision lots were selling, so the goats had to be sold. Next, Mac and Webb bought the adjoining two hundred acres. This land had originally belonged to Ephriam Toungate and his wife, Ann, who was a daughter of Wiley and Catherine Hudson. It had been abandoned like so many of the properties that once had been farmland along the river.

On this very beautiful, undeveloped lakefront property, the two partners attempted unsuccessfully to raise turkeys. Mr. Webb did research on turkeys, and my father built the requisite pens raised off the ground. Together they bought the young turkeys. An army surplus tent was installed on the waterfront property, and a man was hired to live in the tent and care for the turkeys. The man, recovering from tuberculosis, had been told by his doctor to move from the city to the country. One stormy weekend, a kayak washed up on shore, much to my delight and especially to the delight of the man hired to live with turkeys. On weekdays, he began to row across the lake to Dodd City. The community became Volente when Mrs. Dodd applied for permission to have a post office in the little settlement. It seems there was already a Dodd City, Texas. As the turkeys were beginning to die, the caregiver began making more trips to Dodd City. One day, he went missing from the turkey farm, or what was left of it. Mac learned from friends on the north shore that the man had courted and married the widow Mrs. Dodd.

The vacant Toungate land, bought by McIntosh and Webb, was held by their families for more than twenty years. In 1979, it was Hugh Webb's grandson Charles Webb who bought my father's half interest and sold the land to Jim Vier. The attractive Woods of Lake Travis subdivision was created by Vier and partners. Evelyn Webb, daughter-in-law of my father's partner, lived in that subdivision until her death at age ninety-five in 2013. The failed turkey farm is now the subdivision's waterfront park.

Lakeway, founded in 1963, became a city in 1990. In the beginning, there were fewer restrictions and amenities. I remember questioning a friend who invited us to see their new Lakeway land: "Should we bring our Coleman lantern?"

Although there are still many vacation homes in western Travis County, the establishment of the city of Lakeway radically changed the area from its rural beginnings. At first, Lakeway was a vacation and retirement community. Now, it welcomes families and permanent residents and is a thriving city. For a complete history of the founding of Lakeway and its development, I recommend Dr. Lewis Carlson's book *Lakeway: A Hill Country Community*. It was produced for the celebration of the city's fiftieth anniversary.

Today the Hudson Bend Road, leading to our subdivision and others, is populated with commercial development, much of which is unsightly. However, inside the various subdivisions in "the Bend," there are many lovely, permanent, full-time residences. There are no more Angora goats or turkey farms, although University of Texas professor David Crews established a turtle research project on property near Travis Landing and

McIntosh Cove with sailboats moored in the center and swim platforms along the shore. *Author's collection.*

adjoining our subdivision. In 1970, my parents sold their weekend lake house on Pool Canyon Cove and built another modest retirement home on a tract of land overlooking McIntosh Cove. In the cove named for my father, sailboats are moored, and there are a few swim docks. On the streets in Hudson Bend Colony, school buses pick up and deliver children to and from the Lake Travis schools. In 1988, the Hudson Bend Colony Neighborhood Association (HBCNA) was established to curb encroachment of commercial projects into our residential neighborhood. It is still active, but today its activities are more social.

Jesse James's boat docks, at the end of Hudson Bend Road, passed through four owners, two bankruptcies and much reorganization. Today, the three-hundred-slip Lake Travis Marina is a private marina with boaters owning their slips. At one time, Vance Naumann, president of the board of directors, and two more directors were sailboat owners. Despite being outnumbered on the board, Walter Wendlandt and Hal Whiteside reminded us that the marina was a powerboat marina with only twenty sailboat slips. The marina is governed by officers elected by the association of owners. For the last twenty-eight years, it has been managed by Hudson Bend Colony residents Jim and Liz Chapman. Jim's vast experience on Lake Travis, as well as his early work in the North Sea, has made Chapman Marine Service the go-to service for the many marinas on our fluctuating lake. As the lake falls and rises, marinas and docks must be moved constantly. Private boat docks are popular, but they make very little sense on a lake with levels that fluctuate.

With so many people moving to Austin and Central Texas, city life is encroaching. The once pastoral and sparsely populated hill country has become a bedroom community to Austin, one of the fastest-growing cities in the United States.

Weekenders, Cabins and Cottages

At the end of the Hudson Bend Road, the two subdivisions called Hudson Bend Colony and The Reserve at Hudson Bend replaced Joe and Emeline Williams's seven-hundred-acre farm on the river. In 1939, the farm was purchased for $9,000. The old farmhouse was taken down, approximately half of the farm was inundated by the new lake and the remaining acreage was divided into many lots and tracts.

In the early 1950s, Jesse James built the Lake Travis Lodges, as well as boat docks and a small store on an undeveloped tract of land in Hudson Bend Colony. He sold gasoline, bait for fishermen and a few provisions needed by weekenders. The rock cabins were flooded several times and no longer exist. In 1961, one of the lodges on higher ground was rented by the Austin Sailing Club, which became the Austin Yacht Club. The weekend sailors later purchased Beacon Lodges for their permanent location at the mouth of Pool Canyon Cove. Both Jesse's store and the yacht club's first lodge were located on twenty acres of land overlooking Jesse's boat docks. Today, a large, unoccupied home exists on that property. The boat docks in the cove below have been replaced by the Lake Travis Marina, with three hundred privately owned boat slips, including twenty sailboat slips.

Also in Hudson Bend was Brillville on Paradise Cove. Arno Brill's daughter Nellie married Texas governor John Connally. Brill had a ranch from which a fishing camp was created, with cabins to rent and boat docks where weekenders could store their boats during the workweek. Sue Heatly remembers going there as a child with her family on weekends. The oak trees

Brillville as it exists today. The 1950s fishing camp has been converted to rental cabins on Rocky Ridge Road overlooking Paradise Cove on Lake Travis. *Author's collection.*

have been lost to oak wilt, a disease prevalent today in our area of Texas. In 1995, when Sue and I visited what had been Brillville, the bathhouse and gravel drive were gone, but some cabins still existed.

Margaret Olle Womack remembers going through the bump gate on the McCormicks' ranch to get to her parents' lakefront property at the end of Eck Lane. Ed Olle, a former athletic director for the University of Texas, used railroad ties to build his family's weekend cabin. After the dam was finished, the rail line that carried materials and equipment to the dam was taken apart, and the wooden ties were sold to whomever had a use for them.

Friends of Bess and Ed Olle bought Eck Lane lots on the cliff with dramatic views of the new lake. Among them were "Ox" and Ezma Higgins, whose C&S Sporting Goods business in Austin became Rooster Andrews Sporting Goods. A popular surgeon, Dr. Sandy Esquival, and his family traveled the twisting, narrow dirt road to their weekend house. Also on Eck Lane were the weekend lake houses of Dr. Claude Matthews; his wife, Jane; their daughter, Betty; Jane's brother, Bob Yaney; and the editor of the *Austin American Statesman*, Colonel Tom Green and his wife. Most of these buildings were uniquely early Lake Travis weekend homes, built by local tradesmen using native stone and surplus World War II materials from army barracks or Quonset huts and recycled materials like the railroad ties.

Waterfront property on the new lake also was purchased for investment. In the 1940s, $200 could buy a lakefront lot in Hudson Bend Colony. In that subdivision, on an unpaved street later named Lakeshore Drive East, three good friends invested in lots. They were Judd Miller, Claude Voyles and prominent Austin attorney W.W. Heath, who was appointed ambassador to Sweden by President Lyndon Johnson.

Judd and Marian Miller built a lake house on their lot. With their two boys, they enjoyed their waterfront property for many years. I remember water skiing behind young Judd Miller's aluminum fishing boat near the dam where the lake was wide and smooth. The huge Johnson outboard motor lifted the bow of the boat completely out of the water.

Another early and well-known Hudson Bend Colony lot owner was racecar competitor A.J. Foyt of Houston. He built a waterfront vacation home next door to the full-time residence of his friend and mechanic Jimmy Finger. These homes and many others built below the 714-foot spillway level were too close to the lake. Consequently, residents had floodwaters in their houses in 1991.

In the early years after the war ended, there were few places for weekenders to dine. Johnson's Trading Post in Bee Cave had a long history of good food and cold beer. I remember my father ordering a delicious barbecued cabrito from Tom Johnson for a party he and my mother gave. If going into Austin from the upper reaches of Lake Travis, the Trading Post was the place to stop. For those with lake houses closer to the Dam, it was the Marshall Ford Bar and Grill.

For several years, a Hudson Bend Colony neighbor owned and operated La Hacienda Restaurant. It was conveniently located at the corner of Ranch Road 620 and Hudson Bend Road, where today there is a convenience store with gas pumps. Mr. Walsch's very popular restaurant was decorated with fishnets and seashells, and customers were served fried catfish and TexMex food.

Joe and Rosie Arriaga cooked at Johnson's Trading Post until Rosie founded her own business. Her TexMex food was so good and her business grew so fast that she kept remodeling and enlarging and finally moved to the corner of Highway 71 and Ranch Road 620. There she attracted her regulars, weekenders and the many retirees moving into Lakeway during the late 1960s. She closed her Rosie's Tamale House locations in the city of Austin and passed the baton on to another generation in a newer location on

Johnson's Trading Post was located on Highway 71 in Bee Cave and was the go-to watering hole, especially for those with property south of Hudson Bend. *From left to right*: Buck Avery, Lucille Avery, Jim Rodgers, Elizabeth Rogers and Virginia "Billie" Schneider. *Courtesy Ann Johnston Dolce.*

Highway 71. Occasionally, Rosie is there to greet her loyal customers, who include Willie Nelson, and I suspect she still controls what goes on in the kitchen to ensure the same delicious Mexican food as was always available.

On Ranch Road 620, master chef Jeff Blank established the five-star restaurant Hudson's on the Bend near his cooking school and home on Hudson Bend Road. It's a favorite destination restaurant for upscale dining in a rock cottage surrounded by herb gardens. Austin natives, Lake Travis residents and tourists who arrive in limousines enjoy a unique menu in a relaxed setting. Years ago, at a dinner party hosted by another chef, Anne DeBois, I had my first delicious tidbits of fried rattlesnake. Try it—you'll like it.

Another favorite destination restaurant for visitors is Beau Therioux's Oasis. It seats 2,500 people on the multiple levels and decks. One can enjoy Mexican food, margaritas and live music while watching the sunset from a cliff high above Lake Travis. In the uniquely decorated complex, there are other restaurants, a parking garage and gift shops.

A very handsome restaurant with a view of the lake is the Steiner Ranch Steak House. It's located high on a hill that can be seen from Ranch Road 620. Look for the Steiner Ranch subdivision signs. There is valet parking, an open-air terrace and bar and delicious steaks cooked for your delight.

Our neighborhood restaurant is the popular Los Pinos on Hudson Bend Road. Chef and owner Margarito offers a variety of good food. The spinach and mushroom enchiladas with cream sauce are like French crêpes.

Today, there are many good restaurants and fine shopping establishments that cater to our changing community. There is still evidence of what I call the real Lake Travis, but the city encroaches. Developers and contractors are busy creating new subdivisions and building new homes and apartments in and around Austin to accommodate its fast-growing population.

The pace of home building began on a much more modest scale after the end of World War II. At that time, just as today, there were many homes being constructed in the newer parts of Austin. However, there were far fewer subdivisions of homes that were predesigned from which to choose. At that time, one shopped for a lot, selected an architect or designer, engaged a contractor and then waited until materials were available. The lot my mother selected while my father was away during the war was located in Tarrytown on the western edge of town defined by Lake Austin. Because the contractor had speculated a move-in date of September 1949, we decided to spend a leisurely three months at Lake Travis.

Our weekend house on Pool Canyon Cove was not entirely finished, but we packed our goods, stored our unneeded furniture and moved to the lake for the summer. However, we were still there at Christmastime and beyond. I remember very fondly Christmas 1949 at Lake Travis. Because all of our ornaments were in storage, we popped corn to make a garland for our tree and used foil and bright-colored papers to make ornaments.

Still at the lake on a cold February evening, it snowed. The next morning, in my extreme excitement over such a rare Texas event, I persuaded my father to drive us down to look at the waterfront before leaving for school and work. As director of gas utilities for the state, his car had been issued to him by the Texas Railroad Commission. It became hopelessly stuck for two days in the fresh snow in front of our lake house. We used our old 1940 Chevrolet, leaving Mother snowbound and stranded during the day. Driving home in the evening, the nine-year-old automobile could barely climb the steep hill on Ranch Road 2222.

Eventually, we were back in town in our new home. I acquired my driver's license, and finally my mother had a new car to drive. I could

The McIntosh weekend house located on Pool Canyon Cove in February 1949, during a rare Central Texas snow. *Author's collection.*

Austin High School girls swimming in the lake. *Clockwise, starting at lower left*: Carole McIntosh, Alison Gray, Patsy Ludwig, Claire Caswell and Mary Moore. *Author's collection.*

borrow it on occasions to pick up Austin High School friends for drives to Lake Travis and Saturday swims in Pool Canyon Cove. If my parents were there at our lake house, we often had bridge lessons from my card-playing mother.

I remember an almost daily routine one summer. Several good friends and I decided to take a morning summer school chemistry class at Austin High School, after which we would crowd into Suzanne Ashford's chartreuse Ford convertible. Our destination was Eck Lane and the Olles' Lake Travis house. Our lunch consisted of tuna fish sandwiches and Dr Peppers, followed by an afternoon of sunbathing on their dock. Because it was a weekday and we were alone at the lake, we were free to engage in teenage rebellion, secretly smoking Pall Mall cigarettes.

Many years later, after my marriage to Charles and the birth of our two children, we traveled from town to the lake almost every Sunday evening. My parents were full-time residents living in their new Hudson Bend retirement home on McIntosh Cove, and my husband's parents had a weekend house nearby on Hudson Bend Road. Our young children looked forward to Sunday evenings with their grandparents and swims in the lake.

The house with a view that was home to the McIntosh and the Sikes families. *Author's collection.*

Today, in the McIntosh house, we gather with yet another generation—our children's children. On that same porch, we enjoy the same view of the island in the lake that once was a hill on the opposite shore of a river. Living in the footprints of Native Americans and early settlers, it remains possible to appreciate the past and wonder at the future.

Part Three
People and Places—
Interviews and Comments

Today, in the twenty-first century, there are descendants of Wiley and Catherine Hudson still living in areas in and around Austin. Three nineteenth-century Texans who bore the name of the first settlers of Hudson Bend were J.W. Hudson, principal of Fannin College in 1899; Green Hudson, a member of the Travis Rifles, who died in hospital in the spring of 1862; and J.E. Hudson, a member of the Capitol Guards organized on February 22, 1862.[26]

Interviews about more Hudsons were recorded by J.M. "Mulky" Owens and can be found in the Texas Historical Commission Archives. A few are transcribed below.

Interviews by J. M. Owens
March 3, 1970

Talked to Preston Stewart at the Teck Cemetery today about Hudson Bend. He suggested that I talk to Henry Hudson in Austin; Wiley Hudson, Cypress Creek; Ida Stewart, Leander; and John Hudson, Dripping Springs. These are all living children of J.A. Hudson. He confirmed that J.A. Hudson, who is buried in the Teck Cemetery, was the son of Wiley Hudson and that the J. is for Joseph.

He said that a number of the graves in the Teck Cemetery were moved out of a cemetery in Hudson Bend before Lake Travis was formed. J.A.

Hudson's was one of these. The Teck School was just toward the dam from the cemetery. Also confirmed that the school in Hudson Bend was at the head of the draw that is alongside Paul Keller's place.

When I got home, I called Wiley Hudson on the Anderson Mill Road (Cypress Creek). He is a son of J.A. Hudson and said that his father's name was Joseph Alexander Hudson. He suggested that I come by sometime and he would tell me all about those folks. He thinks Mrs. Stewart probably knows more about the family than anyone else.

March 4, 1970

Talked with Mrs. Ida Stewart today. She is the Aunt Ida mentioned by Preston Stewart yesterday. She lives with her son, Harold Stewart, about one mile east of Leander. She is eighty-three years old, very sharp and remembers much about Hudson Bend.

She told me that there was no use talking to John Henry Hudson in Austin, as he does not remember too well. She said that Wiley Hudson at Cypress Creek was younger than she but probably would not remember too much about the bend.

She thought that her brother, John, at Dripping Springs would be the best of her brothers to talk to. He has a ranch on the south side of U.S. 290, about three miles west of Dripping Springs. I stopped there this afternoon, but there was no one at home. Will try again sometime.

She said that her father, Joseph Alexander Hudson, who filed his certificate of occupancy in July 1881, left the Hudson Bend and moved to Hamilton, Texas. His wife and her mother are buried in Hamilton. The father and his family moved back to the Hudson Bend area in 1900. They did not live in the bend but moved to the other side of the river.

She said that the Bee Cave Hudsons and the Round Rock Hudsons are cousins of hers. This further confirms that John Hudson and Edward Hudson, the Civil War chaplains buried in the Old Round Rock Cemetery, are sons of James Hudson, the father of Wiley Hudson, both in the 1860 Travis County census.

She said that Aunty Em (Emeline) married a Williams and that Aunty Jane married Tom Sylvester. This is the T.H. Sylvester who owned land in Hudson Bend.

She said that James Hudson in the 1860 census was her uncle, that his name was James Franklin and that they called him Uncle Frank.

She said there were other children in addition to those in the 1860 census for Wiley Hudson. She did not recognize the names of Caza and

Jeoinetta. She said that she had been told that her Grandfather Wiley Hudson fought in the Civil War and that he made it back as far as Austin, where he died. She said that she wanted to go to the State Cemetery and see if he is buried there.

I told her that I would check on it. He is not.

March 5, 1970

Talked to John C. Hudson today. He lives four and half miles west of Dripping Springs on the south side of U.S. 290. He is the son of Joseph Alexander Hudson who is buried in the Teck Cemetery and is the John Hudson whom Preston Stewart told me about. His mother was Tophenia Harris. She died in Hamilton, Texas, from pneumonia shortly after the birth of his brother Wiley and is buried in Hamilton.

He said that his sister, Alice Hudson Cooper, had the biggest family. He said that she raised ten children and at her death she had thirty grandchildren. She is buried in the Teck Cemetery.

The place where Jesse James lives was his Grandpa Harris's place.

He named some of the people whom he remembered in Hudson Bend: Crumley, Jolly, Toungate. He said that Ephriam Toungate married his father's sister Aunt Ann, and they called him Uncle Eph.

He said that Aunt Em (Emeline, his father's sister) saved her money and that it was in silver dollars, which she hid on a shelf. A man by the name of Charlie Morrison ran off with her money, some said to South America. At any rate, they never heard from him again. Aunt Em's husband was Joe Williams.

He said that there was another Hudson living in Hamilton by the name of Aaron Hudson and that he had the largest family—fifteen children. His father said that he didn't know how Aaron ever fed the family, as he liked to drink and spend his money on liquor. In spite of this, they seemed to eat as well and get along as well as any other family.

He confirmed that the Hudsons in Round Rock and Bee Cave are cousins of theirs.

He said that his Grandpa Harris came from Ireland and that he went to California during the gold rush of '49. While there, he and his partners struck some pretty good pay dirt. They were attacked by Indians and lost all of their gold. When Owens asked him about Defeat Hollow, he related the more accepted story of the stranger on the bluff, calling out and frightening the Indians away because they thought help was arriving.

Ernest "Tubby" or "Sonny" Stewart
Lake Travis View interview by author, September 1995

A tall, broad-shouldered man, who looks even taller beside his diminutive wife, Joy, arrived at the appointed hour for our lunch and interview wearing a traditional country straw hat. My first comment was, "Why on earth did my father call you 'Tubby?'"

"Well, I used to weigh three hundred pounds!" replied Ernest (also known as "Tubby" or "Sonny") Stewart.

Ernest and Joy live near Ranch Road 620 and Stewart Road on Hurst Creek property carved from land that belonged to his ancestors. In the 1860s, Benjamin and Sara Stewart arrived with others who settled this part of the Colorado River. The rich bottomland grew corn and cotton. Ernest remembers the big pecan trees along Hurst Creek on his grandfather Albert Kendrick Stewart's farm and estimates one to have been eighty feet tall.

"When the lake is low, you can still see the tops of many of those trees," he said.

Cutting and clearing for the new lake began at the 635-foot contour level up to 670 feet, leaving the trees in the deepest parts of the lake. The dam's spillway was originally planned to be at the 670-foot contour line and was raised to 715 feet after the dam was underway.

[Sometime before] 1939, there was a flood on the river. With good reason, there was much concern that the unfinished dam might be washed away because floodwaters had twice broken the Tom Miler Dam in Austin.

Ernest Stewart was born in 1924, raised in Austin and spent his summers visiting grandparents and cousins on the Colorado River. Before his mother and father moved back to Lake Travis in 1948, they owned and operated an attractive, contemporary motel on South Congress that is still in existence. The Congress Avenue property on which the motel was built had been purchased by Ernest's maternal grandparents, the Ecks. Although Eck Lane and Teck Cemetery are located on the west side of 620, Grandfather Eck's ranch was on the east side running down to the river below the dam. There was a river crossing below the present low-water bridge that was used by the Ecks when going into town for provisions.

"When Lake Austin is lowered once a year, you can see the bedrock where the Ecks made their crossings," he said. "The banks were too steep for big wagon loads, but this crossing saved about an hour's ride off the trip into town over the easier crossing at Marshall's Ford. The old road to Marshall's

Ford can still be seen if you turn into Commander's Point Road and then to the end of Agarita Drive…look in the direction of the Sometimes Islands about a half mile above the dam." Stewart added, "The trip could be done in one long day; however, Grandpa Eck probably stayed overnight in town."

Ernest remembers his grandparents saying that the crossing over Barton Creek was the most difficult. He also was told by his grandparents that in a canyon, known as Defeat Canyon near the Sometimes Islands, the last skirmish between the Comanche Indians and settlers in the area took place. The Indians agreed to stay in the flint rock foothills and bluffs along Comanche Trail, and the settlers took the bottomland on the other side of the river.

I asked Ernest about the old cemetery that had been below the Hudson Bend Colony subdivision. He never heard anyone say where those graves were moved. However, it's his belief that burials from Graveyard Point were moved to high ground, creating Teck Cemetery.

Like the street Eck Lane, Teck Cemetery was named for Ernest Stewart's mother's family. Somehow, Grandfather Leonard Tilden Eck's middle initial, "T," merged with Eck on the sign above his store and post office. The entire area became known as Teck. All the spaces at Teck Cemetery have been taken, so Ernest and Joy helped create the newer Hudson Bend Cemetery located on the hill off Ranch Road 620, above the new bridge, probably overlooking what had been Grandfather Eck's land.

Earnest continued, "There was a Church of Christ located where Teck Cemetery is now. My grandfather Stewart built a school on the property next to it where Iguana Grill is now. My mother and father both went to that school…but it began to fold after 1937, when the people were moved out for the lake…there wasn't anyone left to go to the school. But the first county school was on a small tract of land located in the middle of your [Hudson Bend Colony] subdivision."

Author's note: The county school tract to which Stewart was referring is currently at the end of a road named Pool Canyon Cove, formerly called Dead Oak Trail. It is now almost landlocked by surrounding lots. There was a dedicated road leading to the abandoned school tract that was not cut when other roads in the subdivision were. There is no evidence of remains of a building on the site. I suspect that the surrounding lot owners will be surprised to learn that the school tract is there, perhaps believing it to be part of their property. I inquired of the county, but it found no record of owning the land.

Ernest believes that perhaps school was taught in temporary lean-to buildings or in tents until the children were sent to the Teck School that his grandfather built. The new school had two classrooms, one for younger and one for older students, with a cloakroom in between and separate outhouses or privies at the rear of the property.

In 1961, Ernest Stewart returned from the city to the land that he remembered as a child, to become the third manager of the newly formed Travis County Water District 17. He said, "In the beginning I was running a one-man operation; reading the meters, sending the bills, and keeping the plant operational." But that is quite another interesting story.

Pat Kimbrough

Lake Travis View interview by author, December 1995

All who knew Pat Kimbrough knew a delightful man with numerous stories that he loved to tell about his days in Hudson Bend. In 1995, I interviewed Pat in Chatters, a dark and dreary restaurant and bar. Previously, it was Three Points, Otis and Ada Benson's beer and bait shop. Later, it was the unofficial office for conducting plans for our new water district and, finally, today's popular Los Pinos Restaurant on Hudson Bend Road.

I should have known to take our truck, instead of my car, to the interview. My Honda was dwarfed by all the macho pickups in the Chatters parking lot. However, our 1978 truck, built before the Datsun factory learned about obsolescence, might have looked even more out of place than the car. When we were seated at our table, I pulled out my new Sony professional tape recorder. Pat, undaunted by the recorder's microphone, filled our time, but alas, not my tape, with wonderful stories of his experiences around the lake in the 1950s. I had failed to turn the recording level up, so all I had was a hum and my memory to rely on.

Pat Kimbrough was a sailor. He, along with architect Eugene George and sailor friend Bill Carter, built his own sailboat and began sailing in 1952. The roadway on the dam had been closed to traffic during the war, but many sailors and fishermen discovered Hudson Bend and Lake Travis by crossing the river on the low-water bridge and driving up the steep hill on the opposite side. Pat knew all three owners of the bait house near the low-water crossing. Preston Cooper was the first owner. After he went blind, he sold to Bob Whiteside, a local contractor. Ray Carter was the last owner. Pat remembers watching *Gun Smoke* at Bob Whiteside's: "It had to be the first television set in the area. And it was the only place to watch football at the lake."

In 1969, Kimbrough was on the executive board of the Hudson Bend Volunteer Fire Department (HBVFD). He loaned me some old, yellowed copies of the *Lake Travis News*. That paper predated the *Lake Travis View* and was staffed by volunteers. From these reports, I learned the names of those first serving on the volunteer fire department. They were Richard Kimball, J.W. Huskins, Norman Larson, L.A. Turnipseed, B.J. Butler and fire marshal John Stamper. Members at large were Dick Neidhardt and Harold H. Bredlow, who also was the first editor of the *Lake Travis News*. Ladies listed as "front starters" of the auxiliary were Beverly Kimbrough, who, along with Pat, had a home in the Lakeland Hills subdivision of Hudson Bend; Bea Larson; Donna Neidhardt; Bernice Huskins; Ruth Kimball; Madeleine Akin; Cleo Dyer; and Isabel Bredlow.

Well-known Hudson Bend resident Paul Keller was listed as an advisor to the editor of the newspaper. Sonny Stewart, also known as Ernest and Tubby, wrote a column called "On the Sunny Side." In a 1969 issue, there was news of Volente, Jonestown and Cedar Park across the lake on the north side.

A 1972 column, entitled "Hudson Bend," was written by Dean Modgling. She reported that the western corner of Hudson Bend Road and Eck Lane was "changing in a big way." Don Cavness (a state representative) and Joe McMordie (known for his whittling of wooden figures and whose wife taught in Austin's Highland Park Elementary School) were cutting roads for their new Vista Grande subdivision.

Early advertisers were Neidhardt Real Estate; Carl Bible Repair Service; J. Coleman Akin's Studio of Art (later home to UT art professor Ralph White and wife, Ruby); Lake Travis Lodges (which no longer exists); and La Hacienda Restaurant, which was located on the corner of Ranch Road 620 and Hudson Bend Road (now a busy convenience store with gas tanks). The newspaper also noted that Jesse James was in intensive care in an Austin hospital.

Pat concluded our interview with: "In those early days, folks spending time at the lake had to endure inconveniences such as the taste of well water or hauling water from town. There were six party line telephones, unpaved roads, cattle guards, bump gates and cows and goats grazing around the camp houses."

Oliver and Anita Sponberg
Lake Travis View interview by author, August 31, 1995

"In 1940, mine was one of the biggest boats on Lake Travis—sixteen feet! Most were fourteen-foot boats," said the tan, fit, energetic man. "I kept my boat across the lake in a cove near Dodd City…that's what it was called in those days," he said as he waved his hand in the direction of Volente, across the lake from where we were sitting in his Hudson Bend Colony weekend home.

Oliver and Anita Sponberg have been coming to Lake Travis on weekends since its creation. When their gate is open, you can find them enjoying the view from their lake house or from under three beautiful, spreading oaks on the grassy lawn at the water's edge.

"I knew Anita when we were kids," Oliver said. "We were neighbors, and I ran around with her brothers. We were friends. Anita was in a sorority at the university, and they always needed boys…we'd date those girls and dance with them. Later on, many years, we started going together."

Anita Disch Sponberg, daughter of Uncle Billy Disch, for whom the Disch-Faulk baseball field at the University of Texas was named, taught girls physical education in several Austin schools.

"She purchased a lot on Lake Travis in 1947 from her principal at Allan Junior High School." Oliver brought out a map of Lake Travis. "Anita's lot was located between Flat Creek and Cow Creek. After leaving Jonestown, there were seven cattle guards or gates we had to go through."

"It was on the opposite side of the lake, across from the Girl Scout Camp, upstream from Lago Vista," Anita added.

Oliver said, "The local man who helped Anita construct her camp house was Carl Varner. He was a fine man, lived simply, was a jack-of-all-trades."

"What we called a hillbilly in those days?" I asked.

"Well, yes," he admitted.

Oliver said Varner poured the slab for Anita and her mother, who were mixing the concrete in a wheelbarrow. When he was putting up the framework, he discovered that the slab was about four inches higher on one side than on the other. He had to cut each stud a different length to make the roof level. There was no electricity and no water. Oliver told me that he got specifications from the state health department and built a vented privy.

Oliver married Anita in 1949, and they watched the water in Lake Travis recede for seven years during a terrible drought in central Texas. In 1954, Oliver and Anita sold their Cow Creek lake house, bought a waterfront lot in the Hudson Bend Colony for $1,650 and built their present weekend home.

"Three years later, the water went over the house, lifted the roof and took off the siding. We had been accustomed to seeing the lake fall," Oliver said. He and many others on Lake Travis never could have imagined the forty-five-foot rise that occurred in 1957, when the drought broke.

Oliver, a retired wholesale building materials businessman, had the house rebuilt with exterior plywood paneling, using drive screws instead of nails. He bolted the roof joist to the studs.

"When water went over this house again in 1991, it took very little to get it in shape...only damage was glass," he said.

Oliver remembers the call from his neighbor Jimmy Finger, a full-time resident, to alert him. Before Oliver left town for the lake, he called an apartment mover, who sent only two men. Other neighbors, the Dykes and Randals, helped clear the house of furniture. "The last time we walked out of here," he said pointing to his house, "water was
up to our knees. We got everything out except the air conditioners. Jimmy's house went under...and A.J. Foyt had water in his second story.

"Luckily, Anita wanted to make some changes to the house before returning the furniture. The house was empty when a second flood occurred just one month later. Finally, the property was restored with little more than a pressure hose to wash down the walls and ceiling."

I asked Oliver and Anita how they found their Hudson Bend property in 1954. Anita said she remembered seeing the property from a boat. They called a realtor representing Mrs. King of King's Florist in Austin. The Kings owned three adjoining lots. To get to the property by car, there was only a dirt road, which came off the Hudson Bend Road approximately where Hi Line Road is today. Oliver laughed and said they had a choice of the three waterfront lots and had to pay fifty dollars more because of the trees on the lot they chose.

After completing my interview and preparing to leave, Anita, still as graceful and lovely as she was many years ago when she taught me to play volleyball at University Junior High School, rejoined us under the big oak trees with a box of used square nails and an old horseshoe. She said the nails were from Joe and Emeline Williams's old dog run farmhouse that had been located in the middle of the seven-hundred-acre farm on the banks of the Colorado River. From the location and the quantity of nails, Anita had guessed where the old farmhouse had stood even before a Williams daughter visited them on a Sunday afternoon and verified this. The lovely trees under whose shade we were standing on the banks of Lake Travis were the same trees that shaded that old farmhouse on the Colorado River many years ago.

The Reverend Malcolm Riker
Lake Travis View interview by author, May 1996

"Life was simple on the lake then…back in the '60s. Ranch Road 2222 was a two-lane road. There was very little boat traffic, about a fourth as many marinas as today." Reverend Malcolm Riker began recalling the years when he lived in Hudson Bend and founded St. Luke's Episcopal Church.

He told me about a fourteen-hour trip upstream on a pontoon boat to Marble Falls. He and archaeologist Dr. Leslie Caldwell discovered an Indian midden near where the Pedernales River enters Lake Travis. "They are all over the place," he said. "It's where they cooked cactus to eat. The rocks will be blackened or will appear red."

Riker's father was a history professor at the University of Texas. Sermons at St. Luke's were often history lectures, as well theological reflections. The tall, very imposing man with a ready response to just about everything is not the stereotypical church minister. He described the biggest day in his life as the rainy bicentennial Sunday in 1976, when he preached three services at St. Luke's under a flag with thirty-seven stars that had belonged to his great-grandfather. He then left immediately for celebrations at St. Christopher's in Oak Hill, St. Richard's in Round Rock and the groundbreaking at the All Faith Chapel on the grounds of Camp Mabry in Austin.

In 1965, Hallie and Malcolm Riker built a home in Hudson Bend on four acres with one hundred feet of waterfront. Elder son Marcus had graduated from Austin's McCallum High School and was gone, but Christopher attended Dripping Springs schools and graduated from Eanes. There were no Lake Travis schools then.

Five years before moving to the lake, Malcolm was persuaded to start St. Luke's Episcopal Church in a bait house near the corner of Anderson Mill Road and Ranch Road 620. He and those early parishioners later built what he calls a shotgun church on the three-acre hilltop site overlooking Lake Travis, where it stands today. The original church now serves as the office. Retired air force officer Al Gates, with wife, Mary Sue, from Volente, found some local rock masons who did a commendable job on those hot afternoons until they were supplied with some cold beer. Looking at the wall, Malcolm can show where the party began and work started to suffer.

Austin architect Arthur Fehr designed a number of Malcolm's earlier churches in Austin, as well as the shotgun church, before designing the sanctuary and the parish hall. Polkinghorn and Cline designed later additions to the original church after Fehr's death.

"It was a wonderful coming together of many talents of both professionals and volunteers to make a church," declared Riker. "The first organ was an old one, difficult to pump. An inventive person connected it to an Electrolux vacuum cleaner that had to be left outside because it was so noisy. Lois Wible was secretary of the church and she built three altars. Catherine Von Merz, whose husband, Karl, had been a Nazi major, donated her excellent library to the church. Mrs. Frank Duval seemed to turn up with $10,000 on three different occasions for landscaping and building projects. Her ashes are buried in the slab of the church." Malcolm said he didn't think anyone knew this, but now we all do.

Hudson Bend Colony resident Marian Miller and Malcolm bought silk brocaded fabric from a Houston company going out of business. Vestments, alter hangings and a pall for funeral services were made by ladies in the parish.

Malcolm continued, "A brass altar cross was given by Austin business leader Clarence Covert and installed just before his death. Ed Berry secured the huge rock for a baptismal font from Capernaum in the Holy Land. It was delivered in an eighteen-wheeler from the Houston Ship channel. Hanging over the font is the church's original cross made by Colonel Scott and Chip West, who, at my suggestion, bruised it with a chain."

There was a tale of cats, pardon the pun. It seems the cats were invited into the church to catch mice. Evidence of their habitation was left for the choir to find before the Sunday morning service. The mystery of missing purses was solved by detective/priest Malcolm Riker by putting silver nitrate powder on a dollar bill in a decoy purse. The harmless powder won't wash off for several weeks.

Then there was the story of an uninhibited flower child of the '60s who fled Hippie Hollow, the nude beach on Lake Travis, and found the church. With her dope but without her clothes, she rode to jail robed in an acolyte's cassock. (For those unfamiliar with liturgical terms, acolytes are the young people who assist in the services, cloaked in robes called cassocks.)

Starnes Island

Excerpt from *Lake Travis View* column "In Hudson Bend," April 17, 1997

Starnes, also known as Rattlesnake Island, was a favorite picnic place for early Lake Travis sailors, and today it is a destination for party boaters. Probably, those sailors gave the island its nickname. Before Starnes became an island, it was a hill on the Starnes property located across the river from Hudson Bend.

In the 1950s, during a very long dry spell, there was a four-thousand-volt power line running from Volente, then known as Dodd City, out to the island. In May 1957, the nine-year drought broke, and days of heavy rains raised the lake level to almost seven hundred feet. [Lake Travis is considered full at 681 feet.] Sometime during that year, the mast of a sailboat hit the power line, and several aboard were badly burned.

The injured sailors, joined by the Austin Sailing Club, filed suit against the Starnes family. The goal was simply to get the line and poles removed. This was in the days before the profusion of personal injury lawyers. Pat remembers that air force planes on maneuvers over Lake Travis hit the lines (after the power was cut) and took them down. The suit was dropped.

Coincidentally, artist and sailor Ralph White mentions those same power lines in the statement he created for us when I offered him some of my column inches in the *Lake Travis View*.

"With my years of youthful enjoyment on many of Minnesota's ten thousand lakes, the viewing of Texas's Highland Lakes in the early 1940s, as an air force pilot, created an indelible impression. An offer to teach in the Art Department at UT [University of Texas at Austin] undoubtedly influenced my decision to return to Texas."

No, Ralph White was not the pilot who downed the lines, but read on.

"My wife, Ruby, and I kept a sailboat in Big Hollow Cove. With a renewed interest in sailing, an early sail [of ours] included a masthead collision with the power lines to Starnes or 'Rattlesnake' Island."

The Whites' residence is near Commander's Point, which overlooks one of the most beautiful coves in Hudson Bend or anywhere on Lake Travis. It has been known by many names—Greathouse Cove, Marsh's Boat Docks and now Commander's Point.

Steiner Ranch

Excerpts from *Lake Travis View* column "In Hudson Bend," July 29, 1999

In addition to the city of Lakeway to the south of Hudson Bend, there are many subdivisions springing up along Ranch Road 620. Gerald Kucera created the Steiner Ranch subdivision east of Mansfield Dam. It is home to many professionals and families who chose to live in the lake area outside the city limits. The Steiner family's huge ranch has always been prominent in Austin's history. In my youth, Buck Steiner owned and operated a leather boot and saddle store on Lavaca Street in central Austin. Buck, who lived into his nineties when most people didn't, left the ranching to his sons in later years while he tended his store.

When writing my "In Hudson Bend" columns, I had ongoing correspondence with Nancy Hutson. She was curious about the possibility of her husband's family misspelling their last name. Could they have been Hudsons? Many times, the spelling of proper names is changed over the years.

As a result of my e-mail conversations with Nancy, I telephoned Tommy Steiner. I was told that his father, Buck Steiner, raised Nancy's father-in-law, Ben Hutson. Ben was given the name "Humpy" because he rode bulls at rodeos.

Tommy Steiner remembers that Humpy drove a truck full of Steiner cattle to market and didn't return when he was expected. He had taken the saddle horse foreman's daughter with him. Steiner said, "When he finally returned, he told everyone that they [the highway patrol] had turned the radar on him, and it burned up every wire in the truck." Now that was a very creative excuse!

Nancy wrote, "We were just talking last night about getting with Buck to see how much he remembers, but it's not easy with our work hours and with Buck almost one hundred years old now and still going to the shop every day."

According to Nancy, "The Steiner Ranch in Bastrop is a big and beautiful spread, just gorgeous. I love going out there. The family reunion takes place on a river on the ranch every summer. We all just camp out."

I often wonder if Nancy and her husband learned more about Humpy and about life on the 620 Steiner Ranch near our part of the Colorado River.

Fishing on Lake Travis

Excerpts from *Lake Travis View* column "In Hudson Bend," September and December 1995

Fishing was the favorite sport in the days of early Lake Travis. Although occasionally there are fishing competitions, today it is boating on the lake that is the fisherperson's fiercest competition. Hudson Bend resident Milton Taylor, now deceased, launched his boat almost every Monday morning to fish while the water was calm after the weekend sport boaters had left the lake. Attached to the ceiling of his garage was his collection of "gimmie-hats" that weekenders had lost while zooming over the lake. It's amazing that so many hats floated long enough for Milton to retrieve them the next day. It makes one wonder how many hats must be at the bottom of the lake.

In 1999, Hudson Bend resident Glen Jurek paused long enough on the tennis court to tell me that the place to fish was Lake Buchanan, with live bait. He waved his hands about as far apart as a tennis racket is long to imply the size of his catch.

Today, most of the fishing camps are gone, at least in the lake around the Hudson Bend. Brillville and Lake Travis Lodges exist only in memories of the children of those early fishers. Sue Heatly, artist and retired professor of design at UT, can still reminisce about the fishing families at Brillville on weekends in the early 1950s. She remembers the bathhouse with showers, the rental cabins near the office and the bait house. While playing on the boat docks with her sisters, Ann and Mary Gail; brother, Sid Heatly Jr.; and some of the other children of the fishing families, young Sue got a huge splinter in her tiny bare foot. Her mother had to rush her to a doctor in town, a considerable trip at that time, to get a tetanus shot.

Arno Brill's boat docks have become Paradise Cove Marina, just as Jesse James's docks have become the Lake Travis Marina. On the lake today, ski boats, yachts, sailing craft and a few fancy bass boats and pontoon boats for fishing vastly outnumber the early aluminum outboard fishing boats.

Austin Yacht Club

Founded as the Austin Sailing Club in 1951 and incorporated in 1963 as Austin Yacht Club, these first Austin sailors met in public libraries and in members' homes. Later, they leased a meeting place in one of Jesse James's Lake Travis Lodges in Hudson Bend. Early members included Francis "Mac" McIntyre, Hap Arnold, Cliff Price, Walter Moore, Tom Romberg and others. Its first commodore, Frank McBee, formed a committee to purchase Beacon Lodges at the mouth of Pool Canyon Cove on Lake Travis. In 1969, a clubhouse was designed by architect-sailor Tom Leach. Submerged land was purchased from Mary and Paul Keller, and sailboat slips were installed. Our lake is filled with sailboats on every Memorial Day for the overnight Turn-Back Canyon Regatta that began in the early 1950s. The annual Red-Eye Regatta on New Year's Day began on January 1, 1976.

Note: This Austin Yacht Club is not to be confused with the older Austin Yacht Club, which once was located on Lake Austin.

Hudson Bend Volunteer Fire Department

For many years, before professional firefighters were hired, a 140-square-mile area was served by the Hudson Bend Volunteer Fire Department (HBVFD). Included was all of the area from the Comanche Trail south on Ranch Road 620 to Highway 71 and west to Hamilton Pool Road and beyond on Highway 71. There was much camaraderie among the men. They were supported by a very active guild. I remember especially Gladys Weyland calling every year with tickets to sell for the fundraiser. One did not say no or even no, thank you, to Gladys. She simply did not take no for an answer. And I'm sure this was true when she approached the stores, restaurants and professional services that donated prizes for the drawing. Proceeds from ticket sales were used to purchase supplies and equipment for the volunteer firefighters.

By 1996, the volunteer firemen had been gradually replaced by professional firefighters. At that time, Lake Travis Fire Rescue Service was established. There are five stations, and the business offices are located on Pheasant Lane. Several men briefly served as leaders of the department before current fire chief Robert Abbott.

Travis County Water Control & Improvement District #17

In 1958, it was determined that the residents of Hudson Bend should have a water district eliminating the necessity for water wells. On February 28, 1959, a confirmation meeting of elected officers was held at the La Hacienda Restaurant on the corner of Highway 620 and Hudson Bend Road. Colonel E.E. Teers was president; Arno Brill, vice-president; Ada Benson, secretary; and Carl Ming and Grace Caruthers, members at large.

It was decided that three hundred meters would be needed, along with thirty-three miles of pipe. The total startup cost was estimated to be $738,000. A bond for a little over half that amount was passed, money was borrowed from two banks, land was purchased from Mr. Lehmans for $5,000 and, in 1960, the contract was awarded to Joe Bland Construction Company to build the first plant in the cove below Eck Lane for $529,590.

Some of the visitors attending those first meetings were Mr. and Mrs. Ed Greathouse, who owned land in what now is called Commander's Point;[27] Mr. and Mrs. Rittenhouse, who owned Beacon Lodges that is now the Austin Yacht Club; Paul Keller of Austin Engineering, who later was a water board member; and A.C. Stewart.

Several years later, S.C. McIntosh, serving as president of the board of directors, became aware of plans for the new Vista Grande subdivision in Hudson Bend. The subdivision's waterfront park was to be located in the cove across Eck Lane and too near the Travis County Water District's intake system. To protect the district's water from contamination, the WCID #17 directors voted to purchase the underwater property at the end of the cove. Ernest "Tubby" Stewart was hired as the third manager. Directors Dean Modgling and Ada Benson were enlisted to keep minutes and mail monthly bills. The Benson's bait shop became a temporary office and meeting place. It was located where Los Pinos Restaurant is today.

In 1996, a larger, permanent office was built at 3812 Eck Lane in Hudson Bend. The current manager, Deborah Gernes, has served for eighteen years and presides over an office and field staff of fifty-four, including her administrative assistant, Linda Sandlin. There are four campuses, four wastewater facilities and 244,000 miles of pipe. The water district now serves an area from the Comanche Trail to Highway 71 West, including Steiner Ranch, Caslano, River Ridge, Hudson Bend, Apache Shores, Flintrock Falls, Falconhead West and Serene Hills. From serving 300 customer accounts in Hudson Bend in the 1960s, the water district now has 10,500 accounts, serving approximately thirty-two thousand people.

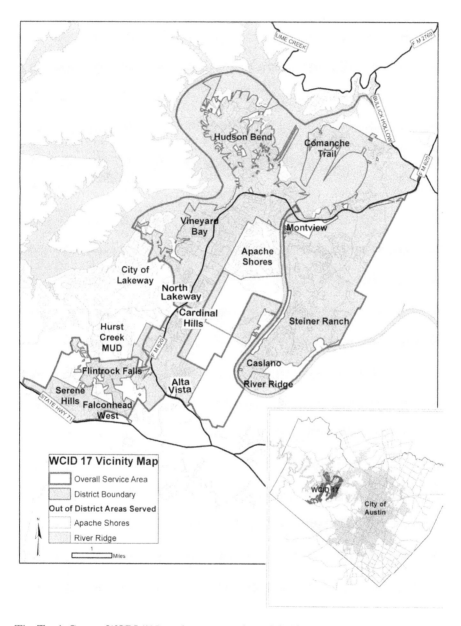

The Travis County WCDI #17 service area, serving subdivisions in the region, 2013.
Courtesy Travis County WCID #17.

Lake Travis Independent School District

Established in 1981, the Lake Travis schools enjoy a fine reputation for scholarship and athletics. Prior to the establishment of the Lake Travis Independent School District (LTISD), children of permanent residents in the areas along Ranch Road 620 made a two-hour bus ride, twice daily, to the schools in Dripping Springs, Texas.

The earliest one-room rural schools in Hudson Bend and Hurst Creek consolidated in 1890 to form the larger Teck school on Ranch Road 620. The exodus of many families, when the lake was created, was the major cause of the Teck School closing about 1937.

The Dripping Springs schools were the only option for children living in the Greater Lake Travis area. In 1969, Lakeway resident Ernest C. Stewart hoped to consolidate Dripping Springs, Eanes and Leander schools into one very large school district. This plan required the construction of a bridge across the lake at the end of Lohman's Crossing, once again connecting the south shore in Lakeway with the north shore of Lake Travis. Stewart's effort failed.

The long ride south into Dripping Springs was impractical for all, but especially difficult for the younger children. Finally, a Lake Travis elementary school on Ranch Road 620 opened in November 1972, ending the difficulties of the long ride for some of the children. After a decade of contention, a split was made with the Dripping Springs schools, and LTISD was formed. A bond issue was voted in 1981 to build middle and upper schools. The district continues to grow and to add schools.

Lake Travis Community Library

The Lake Travis Community Library was given space first in a small school building in the very early 1980s. My Vista Grande tennis friend and Hudson Bend resident Jackie Drees was one of the earliest library volunteers at that location keeping track of books checked out by writing names in a ledger. Later, a small section in the newly constructed Lake Travis High School became the community's library, followed by a move to a shopping center on Highway 620. In 2004, Sue Gilman was the first staff person to be hired. A handsome, freestanding library building was constructed and opened in February 2013 at 1938 Lohman's Crossing. The busy library is staffed with a cadre of volunteers and personnel directed by Morgan McMillian.

Hudson Bend Colony Neighborhood Association

Because in 1988 a young man installed a huge concrete music shell on his parents' waterfront property, the Hudson Bend Colony Neighborhood Association (HBCNA) was founded to discourage commercial activity. While sitting with Clare and Conrad Werkenthin on their deck, listening to some very marginal auditions magnified and wafting across the water in McIntosh Cove, it was agreed that some action should be taken. We learned that our neighbor on the cove had dreams of music events on the grand scale of the Willie Nelson Picnics.

Lawyer Werkenthin gave many pro bono hours creating our neighborhood association. Founding members met to craft our bylaws. The stated purpose for the neighborhood association was "to protect and promote the quality of life and the value of property in our neighborhood." Werkenthin was instrumental (pardon the pun) in having the music shells removed. In the formative years, he and other neighbors served as officers of the board of directors. Like-minded Hudson Bend Colony residents, hoping to discourage commercial development in our residential area

Hudson Bend Colony Neighborhood marker. *Author's collection.*

at the end of the Hudson Bend Road, joined the new association and participated in the annual picnic meetings.

In 1996, a schism occurred between a few property owners in favor of commercial development in the neighborhood and those working to uphold the residential intent of the subdivision. The first group saw an opportunity to challenge the codes by supporting a homeowner who was building a barbecue stand on his lot in Hudson Bend Colony #2. Although there were residential restrictions on the plat of HBC #2, the opposition was hoping to prove that those codes already had been violated.

Ten property owners in that section of the subdivision volunteered to be plaintiffs, and eleven others joined in donating money to hire a law firm. Working with lawyers and the required mediation achieved a settlement. The smokehouse and barbecue stand in Hudson Bend Colony never opened.

There were other challenges. Another important achievement kept the neighborhood from becoming awash with mobile homes. A local mobile home company was planning to purchase vacant lots in the subdivision to sell as a package with his manufactured homes. The owner of the company selected a prominent lot at the entrance to the subdivision. The union of neighbors, who had worked on the barbecue stand project, bought the lot, removed a clutter of signs and advertising and sold the lot for a profit with restrictions for its use. The lot now allows only one large sign directing the way to Emerald Point Marina. This eliminated many of the lost drivers on the streets of our neighborhood who were searching for the marina and the boat rental businesses at the end of HiLine Road.

Members who volunteered to serve as officers and directors in the association over the years are many. Some have died, and others have left. Three former residents who challenged the neighborhood codes have moved. It is especially necessary to say thank you to Erika Rogala and her husband, Stan, founding members who worked to keep the association together during the contentious times.

Among those still in the neighborhood who helped establish the HBCNA by serving on those very first boards of directors are Randy and Eileen Beck, Judy and David Bowen, Martin Holeman, Randy Lacey, Gary and Marsha Paisley, Bobbi and Bill Peace, Jody and Milton Taylor and Carole and Charles Sikes.

Also, thanks to John and Ginger Chapman. They were active in the beginning, then moved away but returned to serve again on the board. There are so many others, too numerous to mention, who have taken leadership roles in the later years. Thank you for that. Fortunately, today's members are enjoying activities more social in nature. The annual picnic is still well attended.

Churches

The churches in our area offer a broader community to their members. I'm told by Lew Carlson that the 2013 Lakeway Residents' Directory lists fifteen churches in our area. The greater area includes Steiner Ranch subdivision on Ranch Road 620 and all those south to Bee Cave and west on Highway 71 to Hamilton Pool Road. I am familiar with only a few of the churches because my husband and I remain active in the church where we were married in the western part of central Austin.

The oldest congregation still in existence in our part of Lake Travis may be the Marshall Ford Fellowship. It is located north of the dam above the big basin of Lake Travis on Marshall Ford Road. My late friend Evelyn Webb, daughter-in-law of my father's partner, Mr. Hugh Webb, was a longtime member of that congregation and an early resident in The Woods of Lake Travis subdivision.

One of the newer churches is Emmaus Catholic Church, on a visible hill in Lakeway. The large church is architecturally fine. It is so tall and imposing that the white cross that stands beside it could not be placed on top of the church because of height limitations. Also in Lakeway, there is the active non-denominational church established many years ago.

Our area around the lake has a rich history of community. The earliest settlers had to depend on one another to survive. Later, residents worked together as volunteers to create and promote many amenities and the organizations on which we depend today. Now our culture seems to encourage being friendlier with Facebook friends and Tweeters than with neighbors. However, there are still ample opportunities to interact with people and have real conversations. There are volunteer jobs and many entertaining events in the area that can be accessed by reading the *Lake Travis View*, *Impact* and *Bee Cave Bee*.

Our churches welcome new members and offer more than Sunday sermons. There are groups for learning and discussion. There are shared meals. Especially if you are new to western Travis County, I recommend some church hopping, and I believe you'll find a community of new friends.

Old Friends Celebrate What Austin Was and Is

Excerpts from *Lake Travis View* column "In Hudson Bend," 1996

Almost every Thursday, I meet for lunch with a group of women who grew up in Austin. We remember the times when we could ride bicycles halfway across town to swimming and piano lessons. We went to the same high school and knew almost everyone in town who was our age.

The Austin of my childhood was a town of about sixty thousand, populated primarily with state government employees, people affiliated with the university and all the small business people it took to support the population. Lake Travis was west of the city, created to control floods, preserve water, produce electricity and provide recreation and enjoyment for the people.

After the Second World War, word was out, and Austin began to grow. Lake Travis became a place to take your boat for a day of fishing or perhaps a place to build a weekend cabin for family and friends to enjoy all year. When the University of Texas students vowed never to leave and more and more people learned about Austin and the hill country, our town became a city.

About twenty years after the creation of Lake Travis, retirees from the military and from all over the world discovered the new retirement development on the lake called Lakeway, and a satellite city was born.

Today, Austin's growth is also making cities of the towns of Round Rock, Georgetown, Buda, Kyle, Bastrop and other surrounding towns. Central Texas is attracting the high-tech community, the film industry, musicians, writers and all manner of entrepreneurs. It continues to be a wonderful place to live and is becoming more diverse and more interesting.

This, in part, is what my friends and I celebrate every week at the Nau's Pharmacy lunch counter in the heart of Austin. Meeting together as we have for about forty years, I confess we complain, with emotion, about the impossible traffic in and about the city. In our youth, we traveled uncongested streets in town and lovely roadways to Lake Travis. We went through bump gates and down winding dirt roads to spend relaxed times swimming, sunning and laughing together. As adults, we participated in our beloved town's progress and cultural advancement. Now, we watch as a new generation grapples with concerns, hoping to find solutions to make Austin a great metropolis.

Notes

Part One
Geography and the River

1. Drinking water in Central Texas is the most critical natural resource that we have. Without water, we perish. Recent droughts and increasing population have compromised our water districts. As citizens are made to curtail their usage of water, the local water utility districts that purify and supply the water are squeezed for revenue to accommodate the numerous new subdivisions of homes.
2. For a delightful and very comprehensive journey down the river, I recommend Margie Crisp's book *River of Contrasts*. Margie is an artist, and she illustrates her book with fine art work and photography as she reveals her knowledge of the geography and of animals, fish, flora and fauna along the river.
3. "This series of lakes is linked together for over one hundred and fifty miles for sports and it is a storehouse of water and a generator of power." Quoted from Barkley, *History of Travis County*, 24.

Hudson Bend: Then and Now

4. Fehrenbach, *Lone Star*.

The Wiley and Catherine Hudson Family

5. "The Wiley Hudson family came to Texas by ox wagon from Missouri in 1837. They settled on a bend in the Colorado River. The community became known as Hudson's Bend and is still known by that today." Quoted from *Kingdom of the Hills Cookbook*, 2nd ed. (Volente, TX: Anderson Mill Gardiners, Inc., 1960), 16.

   "Tasker H. Hudson of Hudson's Nursery of Jollyville told me that this was in the above mentioned cookbook. He said from Tennessee rather than Missouri. He said that the family went back after their first trip to Texas. This could account for the fact that the 1860 census for Travis County indicated that the James Hudson (father of Wiley) family came from Tennessee to Arkansas to Texas. Tasker said that he had heard his elders say that his great-great-grandfather's name was James. He also said that the Round Rock, the Bee Cave and the Hudson Bend Hudsons were cousins. He is the son of the Wiley Hudson who lives at Cypress Creek." From research by J.M. Owens, March 12, 1970, Texas Historical Commission Archives.

6. Fehrenbach, *Lone Star*.

7. Texas Historical Commission Archives.

8. One of three fords used by the early farmers for crossing the river was named Sylvester Ford. It was located near a draw below the place where Cox Springs entered the river on the west side of Hudson Bend. Texas Historical Commission Archives.

9. Texas Historical Commission Archives.

10. Toungate is also spelled Toungat in many of the records. However, I have attempted to be consistent in the spelling here.

11. Texas Historical Commission Archives.

Other Early Settlers

12. I was privileged to know Ernest Stewart, a direct descendant of early arrivals who settled in the Hurst Creek area. He and his wife, Joy, returned to the land that he remembered visiting as a child. He became the third manager of the Travis County Water District #17. He was a great resource for me. An interview with Ernest appears in Part III. It was published in September 1995 in my column "In Hudson Bend."

13. Many of the social activities for the people in early day Hudson Bend were at Nameless and Round Mountain. These two places had a school,

church and a cemetery and were located on the north shore of the river, within horseback and wagon ride distance of Hudson Bend. "Mrs. W.T. Colley, née Barbara Charlotte Lohmann, who was eighty-three years of age in 1970 and is now deceased, told me that there were schools at one time or another at Cox Springs, Hudson Bend, Nameless, Hurst Creek and Teck, and that is where the community socials were held. Her grandfather was the Lohmann for whom the Lohmans Crossing, near present Lakeway, was named, and [she] lived all of her life in the area of Travis County." Unknown author, Texas Historical Commission Archives.

14. In 1931, it was necessary to build an additional room. Cloakrooms and bookcases were added, and the entire building was remodeled and painted. Another milestone was crossed in 1932 with the organization of the Parent-Teacher Association. *Defender*, 1936. See also Barkley, *History of Travis County*.

The Joe and Emeline Williams Farm

15. Nameless School was restored in 2009. Friends of Nameless School began holding fundraisers, quilt sales and raffles to raise money. They also secured two grants, one from the Texas Historical Commission and one from the LCRA. It has had many uses. As well as a school, it was a place for the early settlers to socialize and later a voting site and a place for quilters and others to meet. From Genny Kercheville.

16. I recommend reading Elaine Perkins's *A Hill Country Paradise?: Travis County and Its Early Settlers*. It is filled with colorful stories about the people who settled western Travis County. Elaine is a resident of Bee Cave, Texas. She has collected early photographs of the settlers, their names, their occupations and anecdotes about their lives. The book is entertaining and imparts the stories of the hardscrabble lives of these hill country Texans who settled the land from Hudson Bend to Bee Cave and across the river on the north shore.

17. To learn about Charcoal City and people on the north shore, read *The North Shore of Travis Lake* by the North Shore Heritage and Cultural Society. The book contains stories of Native American groups, people and places, both historical and modern, along the north shore of the river.

18. See the Part III to read about Anita and Oliver Sponberg, who purchased the lot in the Hudson Bend Colony on which Joe and Emeline Hudson Williams's old farmhouse stood prior to 1939, when it was demolished.

Part Two

The Dam at Marshall Ford: Changing Lives

19. Around 1931, a concrete bridge known as Lohmann's Bridge was constructed by C.A. Maufrais and financed by local residents. The cost was $4,000. It connected the north shore with what is now Lakeway. Today, the bridge is under water, as is the Lohmann homestead. Before moving to the hill country, John Henry Lohmann (1799–1891) had a dairy and provided all the milk for the city of Austin. From North Shore Heritage and Cultural Society, *North Shore of Lake Travis*.

20. Lewis Carlson's *Lakeway: A Hill Country Community* is a comprehensive history about the founding of Lakeway in 1963. I encourage you especially to read the first three chapters as a prelude to the stories in this book. Professor Carlson gives a prehistory of the area.

21. With the change in land use due to the construction of the dam and the impoundment of the waters above it, the area changed from farming and ranching to subdivisions. Most of the population consists of now-retired people living in Hudson Bend or commuters from Hudson Bend to Austin and those living in surrounding areas commuting to work. There are still a few people living in "the Bend" who are descendants of the original settlers. Marinas, fishing docks and lodges compose the commercial establishments in the Hudson Bend. There are no stores of any kind actually in Hudson Bend. Notes from Texas Historical Commission, circa late 1940s/early 1950s.

22. For a riveting description of the maneuvering necessary to complete these dams, I recommend Robert Caro's *Path to Power*, Vol. 1. These volumes are a biography of Lyndon Baines Johnson.

23. Mansfield Dam, named for Joseph Jefferson Mansfield, was officially opened in 1943 but began generating electricity in 1941. Built on the Colorado River in Travis County for the Lower Colorado River Authority, it was financed in part by the United States Bureau of Reclamation. The dam impounds Lake Travis, a reservoir covering 41,940 acres. In December 1948, the LCRA and the secretary of the interior signed a contract, as required by Congress in the United States Statutes at Large, LIII (1939), whereby the authority was to reimburse the United States for a part of the expenditures on Mansfield Dam. The amount of the reimbursement was set at $5,510,500. From Walter Prescott Webb, *The Handbook of Texas*, Vol. 2 (Texas State Historical Society, 1952), 137.

World War II

24. This reference is to the new partner in the Hudson Bend Colony project. State treasurer Jesse James bought the two Edwards interests, thereby acquiring the major interest in the subdivision. A solution found after McIntosh returned from the war was to divide all unsold lots and tracts so that all three partners could act independently of one another.

After the War Ended

25. The first civic group to be formed in the Highland Lakes area at the end of World War II was the Lake Travis Improvement Association. Next, the following civic organizations were established at Hudson Bend: The Hudson Bend Garden Club, the Hudson Bend Lions Club (1971) and the Hudson Bend Volunteer Fire Department (HBVFD) From Barkley, *History of Travis County.*

Part Three

26. Barkley, *History of Travis County.*

Travis County Water Control & Improvement District #17

27. "Before it was called Commander's Point, it was Greathouse Cove. A man named Deckard constructed the first dock there. He had worked on the dam, and the story is that he bought some of the surplus materials to build docks. I don't know if that's true. Mr. Greathouse was married to my mother's niece, a member of the Eck family. He worked at the Kennelwood Boat docks on Lake Austin. He also owned some docks on the west bank of Lake Austin, as well as those in Greathouse Cove." From Ruby White.

Bibliography

Books about Texas and Texans

Barkley, Mary Starr. *History of Travis County and Austin, 1839–1899*. Waco, TX: Texian Press, 1963.

Carlson, Lewis. *Lakeway: A Hill Country Community*. Helena, MT: Sweetgrass Books, 2011.

Caro, Robert. *Path to Power*. Vol. 1. Audiobook. Newport Beach, CA: Books on Tape, 1988.

Crisp, Margie. *River of Contrasts: The Texas Colorado*. College Station: Texas University A&M Press, 2012.

Fehrenbach, T.R. *Lone Star: A History of Texas and the Texans*. New York: Macmillan Publishing Co., Inc., [1968].

Kerr, Jeffery. *The Republic of Austin*. Austin, TX: Waterloo Press, Austin History Association, 2012.

North Shore Heritage and Cultural Society. *The North Shore of Lake Travis*. Charleston, SC: Arcadia Publishing, 2010.

Perkins, Elaine. *A Hill Country Paradise?: Travis County and Its Early Settlers*. Bloomington, IN: iUniverse, 2012.

Varner, Byron D. *Lakeway: The First 25 Years—and Earlier Times Around the Colorado River*. Austin, TX: Capital Printing Company, 1988.

Articles, Interviews and Research

Barnes, Michael. "Couple Unites Through History." *Austin American Statesman*, June 30, 2013.

Community Impact. "Lake Travis and Eanes ISDs Undergoing Changes." 2013.

Cox, Mike. "Hudson Bend." TexasEscapes, online magazine. December 16, 2005.

Defender. Publication of the rural schools of Travis County, 1936.

Owens, J.M. "Mulky." "Hudson Bend." Texas Historical Commission Records, 1977.

Sikes, Carole McIntosh. "In Hudson Bend." *Lake Travis View* columns, 1995–98.

Index

INDEX

V

Vier, Jim 46
Vineyard subdivision 53
Vista Grande subdivision 95
Volente 46, 79, 95, 96
Von Merz, Catherine 99
Voyles, Claude 83

W

Watson, James Ray 51
Webb
  Charles 79
  Evelyn 79
  Hugh 20, 46, 55, 60, 70, 72, 73, 74,
      75, 79
Webb Lane 40
weekenders 12, 16, 18, 57, 81, 83, 102
Wendlandt, Walter 80
Werkenthin, Clare and Conrad 107
West, Colonel Scott and Chip 99
Weyland, Gladys 103
Whiteside
  Bob 94
  Hal 80
Wible, Lois 99
Williams
  Emeline Hudson 20, 21, 37, 55, 56,
      57, 90, 91, 97
  Henry 20, 60
  Joe 20, 21, 37, 46, 48, 55, 56, 91, 97
Wirtz, Alvin 65, 67
Womack, Margaret Olle 82
Woods of Lake Travis subdivision
      46, 79
World War II 60, 68, 72, 85

Y

Yaney, Bob 82

Z

Zintincho, George 40

About the Author

Carole McIntosh Sikes, a native of Austin, writes with knowledge and affection about the people who settled along the Texas Colorado River and those who replaced them when the river became a lake.

She is recognized in the Archives of Women of the Southwest in the DeGolyer Library at Southern Methodist University in Dallas, Texas. Writing projects include "In Hudson Bend" columns for the *Lake Travis View* and two books, *Fairy Tales Are Real* and *Growing Up in Austin*.

A professional artist and former teacher who loves to write, she was the first woman to earn a master's degree in painting and print making from the Art Department at the University of Texas at Austin. She participates in group and solo exhibitions of her paintings. Awards include a purchase prize from the Tyler Art Museum and those given by the Texas Fine Arts Association.

She lives with her husband at Lake Travis, in Hudson Bend, on land her family purchased in 1939. They enjoy five grandchildren who live in Austin and Dallas.

CPSIA information can be obtained
at www.ICGtesting.com
Printed in the USA
LVHW101150080320
649309LV00083B/728